HOW TO MAKE YOUR MAN LOOK GOOD

(Without Making Him Feel Bad)

HOW TO MAKE YOUR MAN LOOK GOOD

(Without Making Him Feel Bad)

Nancy Butcher

A Perigee Book

A Perigee Book
Published by The Berkley Publishing Group
A division of Penguin Putnam Inc.
375 Hudson Street
New York, New York 10014

First edition: May 2002

Visit our website at www.penguinputnam.com

Library of Congress Cataloging-in-Publication Data

Butcher, Nancy.
    How to make your man look good : (without making him feel bad) / by
    Nancy Butcher.
        p.   cm.
    ISBN 0-399-52754-0
    1. Man-woman relationships.   2. Grooming for men.   3. Men—Health
and hygiene.   4. Communication—Sex differences.   5. Persuasion
(Psychology).   6. Influence (Psychology).
I. Title.

HQ801 .B888   2002
306.7—dc21
                                                              2001036871

Printed in the United States of America

10 9 8 7 6 5 4 3 2 1

For Jens

Contents

Acknowledgments

This book would not have been possible without Ken Siman at Penguin Putnam.

I would also like to thank my editors at Penguin Putnam, John Duff and Tess Bresnan; my agent, Susan Cohen; and others who helped along the way: Hollace Beer, Andrew Grec, and everyone at the Creative Bloc.

I want to express my sincere gratitude to the health, wellness, fitness, style, and beauty experts who allowed me to interview them for this book: Dr. Mark Goulston, Jeanine Barone, Regina Cornell, Noah Pacifico, Dr. Ken Goldberg, Alan Flusser, Glenn O'Brien, Marvin Piland, John O'Malley, Dr. Mary Ellen Brademas, Dr. Frederic Brandt, Brad Johns, Anne Greene, and Todd Norian.

A very special thanks to John McPherson for his wonderful cartoons, his friendship, and his support.

And to all those men and women out there who shared their stories with me—thank you, thank you, thank you.

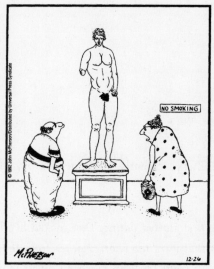

"I wish you'd renew your membership
at the health club."

Staplers, Spare Tires, and Studs
(The Good Kind)

My friend Cheryl recently told me a story about her ex-husband, Dan*:

> When we first started dating, Dan looked like hell: frayed shirts, pants that were too short, clothes from the 1970s that his mom had bought for him. It wasn't an issue of money. I guess he thought he looked "funky" or something.
>
> Anyway, on our second date, he took me to a really nice restaurant in a hotel. On our way in, he stopped in the lobby and asked the clerk for a stapler—then proceeded to staple the holes in his pants pockets as well as the hem of his overcoat. I was perplexed, to say the least!

Okay, so maybe we don't all go out with guys who have to staple their clothes on a date, but if your man is like many men out there, he could probably use some improvement in the ap-

---

*These are made-up first names, as are the names of all the men and women whose stories appear in this book. This is to protect their anonymity. However, the names of the health, wellness, fitness, style, and beauty experts—who are also mentioned in the acknowledgments—are real. So is the name of my six-year-old son, who insisted on being in this book (and who insisted that the title should be changed to *How to Make Your Boy Look Good*).

pearance department, whether we're talking wardrobe, physique, or general grooming. Maybe his love handles aren't so loveable. Maybe he hasn't trimmed his toenails since the Reagan administration. Maybe you wish he'd wear something other than his I'M WITH STUPID T-shirt once in a while.

You want your man to look and feel his best. The problem is, how do you help him get from *here* to *there*? Unfortunately, even the slightest nudge in that direction—whether it's a gym membership tucked into his Christmas stocking or a well-meant comment like "Honey, maybe you should think about getting a haircut"—can set off fireworks. The wrong *kind* of fireworks. Your man can feel defensive instead of motivated, nagged instead of grateful.

So how do you break through that barrier and help him achieve the state of optimum health, fitness, and style that he deserves?

This book will show you how, using a positive, holistic, "man maintenance" plan that emphasizes well-being, togetherness, nurturing, and most of all, fun.

W*hy* did I write this book? Because it's the book I wish I had myself, years ago.

I once had a significant other I will call Antonio. Antonio and I were together for a decade. Over the course of that decade, we went through our ups and downs. But one of the more striking "downs" was the way I handled—or rather, mishandled—the issue of his appearance.

Antonio was pleasantly attractive. When I first met him, he was working in an office, so he dressed well every day: nice slacks, nice shirt, nice jacket or cardigan. He wasn't exactly a fashion plate, but he looked just fine, and he had enough interesting accessories—vintage ties, a pair of designer glasses that cost more than a month's rent—to elevate his look a notch above "ordi-nary."

We eventually moved in together. Antonio quit his job and began working from home, which meant he didn't have to get up, get dressed, and "go into the office" every day.

During this phase, Antonio stopped getting regular haircuts. His daily uniform became ratty sweats and T-shirts. He gained a lot of weight.

My response? I was on him all the time. I glared at him every time he reached for the Ben and Jerry's. I made fun of his sweats and T-shirts in a not-so-playful way. I bought us a couple's mem-bership to the gym and then harassed him daily because he wasn't using it.

In other words, I acted like his mother, and he acted like a rebellious teenager ("I don't *have* to comb my hair if I don't want to!"). Not a pretty picture.

At the same time he was gaining weight, I was losing a lot of it. I actually took advantage of our couple's gym membership. I began eating better: more vegetables and fruits, less sweets and snacks. I bought new clothes to fit my new physique, and I looked better than I had in years.

I could have taken my new healthy habits and attitudes and tried to share them with Antonio in a positive, loving, light-hearted way. Instead, I rubbed it in. "If *I* can find time to go to the gym, you should, too," I accused. "Don't you know that beer has a *ton* of calories?" I pointed out every time he grabbed a cold one.

Antonio and I are no longer together, although we are still friends. One of my biggest regrets is that I couldn't change the negative, supercharged dynamic between us over the issue of his appearance. If I'd just known how, I could have stopped acting like his mother and started acting like his lover and partner. If

I'd just known how, I could have helped him look and feel better in a way that added to—rather than detracted from—our relationship.

Now I know how. Which brings us back to this book.

When I told my women friends that I was writing this book, I was flooded with enthusiastic responses. Everyone seemed to have a tale of woe about her husband or boyfriend that echoed my own experiences with Antonio:

I can't get my boyfriend to wear a tie!
I can't get my husband to lose weight!
My *husband looks like Charles Manson!*

In writing this book, I sent out questionnaires asking women for their own "how to make your man look good" tales of woe as well as their success stories. I talked to a fair number of them as well. I also interviewed professional experts whose business it is to make men (and women) look and feel good.

I also spoke to several men to get *their* side of the story. How do they feel when their women drop hints about "getting more exercise" or "losing that spare tire"? When their women start buying cookbooks with the word *low-fat* in the titles, and suddenly everything on the dinner table involves weirdo foods with names like tempeh and seitan? When their women come home with lavender shirts and matching lavender ties because "Dylan McDermott wore that on *The Practice* last night, and he looked really hot"? When their women say the words "Ow, you just stabbed me with your toenail!" in bed way more often than "Come here, you big stud"?

In order for you to help your man, it's important to understand what works for him—and what absolutely, totally, and undeniably doesn't.

You will find that most of the chapters in this book include two basic chunks of information: what you (and your man) need to know about nutrition, fitness, or whatever is specific to that chapter's topic; and what you alone need to know to apply that knowledge to your man.

As you go through the book, remember that it's all connected. The reason you want to make your man look and feel good is because you love him. (Okay, and because you're tired of seeing him in the same polyester dress shirt from 1981.) The more you express that love to him, the more he will be inclined to express his love for you—by looking his best for you.

It's all connected, too, because one positive change often begets another. Once you can encourage him to make just one positive change, others will follow. If he loses a few pounds and feels more energetic because the two of you are eating pasta primavera by candlelight rather than Taco Bell in front of the tube, he may be inclined to start joining you on your morning run. And seeing his new buff self in the mirror may get him excited about buying some new clothes or getting a new haircut—all of which will probably encourage *you* to say "Come here, you big stud" a lot more often. Which loops us back to the above: He's happier with you, you're happier with him, and the gift just keeps on giving.

Happy reading!

Nancy Butcher
June 2001

Chapter One

Life with a chronic article-clipper.

Why Is It So Hard to Make
Your Man Look Good Without
Making Him Feel Bad?

Maria and Eric, who are both in their 40s, have been married for 12 years. The issue of his appearance is a long-standing battle between them:

> It's not that I want Eric to look like Mel Gibson or anything like that. I love him for who he is—he's a good husband and father. But over the last five or six years, he's really put on the pounds. Maybe it has to do with all his stress at work, I don't know.
>
> For breakfast he'll grab a Danish on the road, and I know he goes to McDonald's for lunch. Whenever I make a comment about that, like maybe he should cut down on the junk food, he just gets mad at me.
>
> I don't even know the last time he exercised. I tried to talk him into joining the tennis league at the Y once, but he got mad about that, too. He said, "I have to work all day, I don't have all that free time like you do."

Like Maria, some women can't even bring up the subject of their man's appearance without provoking a fight. And even if there isn't an outright fight, there can be resentment and resistance. Said one woman: "My boyfriend wears wrinkly shirts and old jeans when we go out. I've told him that it bothers me, but he just keeps doing it. It's become this tense, unspoken *thing* between us. Why can't he dress up once in a while, to make me happy?"

It seems so simple, doesn't it? You care about your man, and you care about how he looks. And you figure that if he cares about *you*, he'll want to look good for you.

But when you try to offer advice—when you say things like, "Honey, that tie doesn't match," or "Sweetie, it's time we got that StairMaster out of the attic for you!"—you get anger instead of agreement. You get attitude instead of gratitude.

Why is it that so many men can feel nagged, criticized, bullied, mothered, or smothered when we try to help them in the appearance department?

It's a man thing

There are many reasons why your man may glare at you when you make comments about his weight or wardrobe or toenail-trimming inadequacies:

• Perhaps he feels that these are "women's issues," and he resents you imposing your "woman's agenda" on him. He's a man, after all, and he's got more manly things to worry about.

• Perhaps he doesn't like change, so the idea of dressing in Calvin Klein (when he's been an L.L. Bean guy all his life) or signing up for spinning classes (when his idea of exercise is casting for trout or playing 18 holes with his buds) doesn't sit well with him.

• Perhaps your comments really *do* remind him of his mother—it's like he's nine years old again and she's yelling at him to clean behind his ears and put on a decent shirt. Chances are, this is not a pleasant or sexy experience for him.

• Perhaps he hears your comments as a criticism of him—i.e., *all* of him. So instead of hearing, "Honey, I'm worried about your weight," he hears, "Honey, you're a total loser."

"A man's self-esteem is often tied to his feeling of competence," says Dr. Mark Goulston. "And his competence is often tied to how much he's in control of his world versus how much his world is in control of him. So often, anything that threatens his sense that he's in control, that he's competent, will rapidly attack his self-esteem."

Dr. Goulston is an assistant clinical professor of psychiatry at UCLA and the author of *The 6 Secrets of a Lasting Relationship: How to Fall in Love Again—and Stay There*. He is also the cofounder of www.couplescompany.com, an e-learning site dedicated to helping couples be as successful in their relationship as they are in their careers.

Of course, it's not just *what* a woman says to her man about his appearance. It's *how* she says it, too.

"You don't want to suddenly surprise a man with your constructive criticism," Dr. Goulston advises women, "because it's often the element of surprise that can turn something that was well-intentioned into something that starts a fight."

Part of the reason is because men and women are wired differently when it comes to processing information and communicating. Men often think before they speak, because they're afraid of saying the wrong thing. Women, on the other hand, speak first and think second, because the act of speaking can actually help them form and clarify their thoughts.

But because of this basic difference, a woman's spontaneous observation—"Gee, that shirt doesn't match those pants"—can catch a man off-guard and make him feel criticized, even if her intentions are good.

Here are some tips from Dr. Goulston on communicating your "how to look good" comments to your man more effectively:

• **Knock before you enter.** Don't just march into the living room while your man is channel-surfing and announce, "Darling, I think we should start exercising together!" "Just because he's sitting there doesn't mean his mind isn't occupied with something," says Dr. Goulston. "Men don't like being surprised. He hears that to mean: 'What I'm saying is more important than what you're thinking about.'"

• **Don't corner him.** Stay away from the grim, serious, "Honey, we need to sit down and have a talk" approach, which can make your man feel like a trapped animal. Says Dr. Goulston: "Make it off-the-cuff. While you're in the middle of some other activity (like driving), so it's not like one of those heart-to-hearts that hits him between the eyes, say: 'What's the best way to bring up something about you that's bothering me so it has the best chance of getting through in a positive way?'" Then, before your man has a chance to respond, bare your own neck. Say something like, "For instance, the best way for you to tell me that I'm acting like a total bitch is for you to give me a big hug and whisper 'I love you, Ms. Cranky' in my ear. That way, I get your point without feeling totally offended." After you've opened up, it's easier for your man to open up, too.

Are Men Half-Brained When It Comes to Listening?

According to a study conducted by a radiology professor at the Indiana University School of Medicine, men use mostly the left sides of their brains while listening, while women use both sides. The left side is associated with logic and objectivity, while the right side is associated with intuition and subjectivity.

• **Don't get into a debate.** Once you're into a discussion about why he won't get his hair cut or why he won't dress up for you, don't negate whatever he says. Be receptive. Dr. Goulston suggests saying something like, "Gee, really? I never would have thought of that. Thank you." A comment like that shows your man that you admire him. It's also a way of turning an awkward situation into a positive one.

• **Finesse his resentment.** If you bring up some appearance issue and your man comes back at you with, "Yeah, well, you always act like you know everything," you need to bite the bullet and say, "I do that a lot, don't I?" Dr. Goulston explains that being gracious is likely to diffuse the situation and make your man want to be on his best behavior. "As difficult as this may be to do, do it," he says. "And then pat yourself on the back."

• **Don't stop halfway.** You can't offer a criticism—constructive as it may be—then leave your man hanging on a limb, feeling like he's overweight or underdressed or otherwise unattractive. "If you bring up a criticism, please bring up a solution," says Dr. Goulston.

It's a woman thing

A woman can bring her own baggage to the table when it comes to talking to her man about his appearance.

For example, if a woman anticipates that a "constructive criticism" conversation might not go well, it can create performance anxiety in her. She might come off sounding naggier and nastier than she meant to.

According to Dr. Goulston, there is a term dog-lovers know: "fearful aggression." It refers to the fact that when dogs get afraid, they growl. Likewise, when a woman is afraid that something she's going to say to her man will be met with a defensive response, she might feel aggressive before the conversation has even begun.

The result? Instead of expressing the fear ("I'm afraid that if I bring up your weight, you're going to yell at me again"), a woman covers it up as aggression.

"Underneath anger, there is almost always fear," says Dr. Goulston. "Anger is almost always an effort to cover up vulnerability."

Being unsure of how to start the conversation can make the woman's performance anxiety even worse. Just as a man's self-esteem is affected if he feels like he is incompetent or not in control, a woman's self-esteem can be affected if she feels that she is not a good communicator. In the end, she can end up feeling extra-vulnerable—and act extra-aggressive.

The solution? Try to recognize that it's fear talking, not anger. Be willing to expose yourself emotionally. Dr. Goulston recommends the following conversation-opener: "You know, there's something I want to point out to you, but I'm really afraid that no matter what I say, it's actually going to make things worse. As a result, I don't know quite what to do. Does that ever happen to you?"

Another kind of baggage a woman can bring to the table is what Dr. Goulston calls the "Scarlett O'Hara" phenomena. Remember her famous declaration in *Gone With the Wind:* "I'll never be hungry again"? If a girl watches her passive mother get steamrolled by her controlling father, she might say to herself, "This is never going to happen to me!" As a result, that girl may grow up to be overly controlling herself—because she's hell-bent on not ending up like her mother. A girl can also grow up to be overly controlling if she had to witness—or endure—other types of out-of-control relationships in her childhood.

A controlling woman is not going to make much headway with her man when it comes to his appearance, because he will have learned long ago to tune her out. He will not like communicating with her and will often respond with one-word answers. On the other hand, she may notice that he's just fine communicating with other people.

It's a lose-lose situation for both the man and the woman. "Often, our adult relationships die for the sins of the relationships we watched in our childhoods," says Dr. Goulston.

If you suspect that you might have control issues—that your wanting your man to shed a few pounds or wear better suits is more about controlling him than helping him—then it's time for you to stop and regroup. Do some serious soul-searching. Consider therapy—and your priorities. Do you want to be ruled forever by your bad childhood? Or do you want to have a loving and lasting relationship with your man?

It's a relationship thing

"When we were first married, Sean always looked put to-gether," says Natalie, age 40. "Even around the house, he would wear nice khakis or shorts and a polo shirt. He'd shave twice a day. After 15 years of marriage, though, it's a whole different story. On weekends, when he doesn't work, he wears grungy clothes, and he doesn't bother shaving. It's like he's saying to me, 'My job matters, but you don't.' "

Generally speaking, says Dr. Goulston, women need to feel cherished in a relationship. Men, on the other hand, need to feel admired.

Like Natalie, a woman's sense of feeling cherished can be shaken when her man doesn't bother to look good for her. Deep down, he may still cherish her. He may be hanging out in sweats just because he's comfortable in them, and he's comfortable around *her*. But that's not how she sees it.

Likewise, a man's sense of feeling admired can be shaken when his woman criticizes his appearance. When she complains about his grungy weekend clothes, he doesn't hear, "I need to feel like I'm special," he hears, "You're a slob."

Recognizing this dynamic is half the battle. Says Dr. Goulston: "Step back and think about it. What's really hurting you, the woman, is the lack of consideration. It was that special consideration that made you feel so wonderful in the beginning. There's a fear that it's gone forever and you can't get it back. That's often painful."

The other half of the battle is communicating what you really feel to your man—and having him get the message. How do you get him to hear, "I need to feel like I'm special" instead of "You're a slob"? How do you stop the tug-of-war of "You don't care!" and "You won't stop nagging me!"?

For starters, Dr. Goulston suggests expressing the following sentiment to your man:

There was a time . . . and I know you like to feel comfortable and be yourself . . . but there was a time in our relationship when I felt really special. And I hope there was a time in our relationship when you felt really special. But lately, there are some things you say and do . . . and I bet there are things I say and do also . . . that have the effect of making me feel the opposite of special. Does that ever happen to you?

Or you could get even more specific:

I sort of had a revelation I wanted to share with you. I used to feel adored by you, cherished by you. I feel like I've gone from being cherished and adored to the opposite of that. I sort of feel like a toilet. I bet that there are a lot of things I do that make you feel the same. I bet you used to feel like you were a blessing in my life, that I looked up to you. I still feel this. But then I begin to think about the things I do that don't make you feel special. Like when I first see you at the end of the day without checking how your day was, and I'm down your throat with my anxieties, like my anxieties take priority over your day.

Of course, if you really *are* down his throat with your anxieties all the time—and that may be contributing to the bad blood between you and making him not want to look good for you—then you need to go one step further. In this case, Dr. Goulston suggests saying something along these lines:

I bet one of the other things I do that makes you feel un-special . . . one of the places where you feel that you've failed most . . . is to make me happy and keep me happy. Maybe I come off as easily irritated or upset or bothered. And I know that you want to feel like you're still the prince who came into my life. I bet one of the places where I destroy your specialness is there. Isn't that true? You probably feel like you're effective everywhere in your life except there.

See a pattern? It's all about getting to the real conversation. Deep down, it's not about his yucky T-shirts and uncombed hair. It's not about your nagging and complaining. It's about two people who love each other—who are afraid that the other person doesn't love them as much as they used to.

But what if your man really *is* a slob?

Maybe your guy's penchant for stained clothes, dirty finger-nails, or Mac Attacks has nothing to do with comfort or casual-ness. Maybe he's a Certifiable Slob. Then what?

If your man was a slob when you began your relationship with him, that's one thing. You knew what you were getting. Can you realistically expect to change him now?

But if your man is a Nouveau Slob, then something else may be going on. The best way to approach him is not to get angry or take it personally, but to put yourself in his shoes.

"You may discover that one of the reasons he's a slob is be-cause he feels like everyone in his life owns him except him," says Dr. Goulston. "There's a part of him that feels that he lives for everyone else, given the responsibilities he feels he has to

Instead of Saying . . .

Instead of saying:

  "Honey, you're getting fat."

Say:

  "I'm afraid if you keep gaining weight, you're going to have a heart attack and leave me and the kids."

Instead of saying:

  "Can't you wear something a little nicer than that?"

Say:

  "I'm scared that the reason you don't dress up for me anymore is because I've stopped being special to you."

carry, given all the masters in his life he feels he has to serve. It may be that being a slob is his way of saying, 'There's going to be something in my life that is just me.' "

If you suspect that's what's going on with your man, don't make a comment like, "I wish you wouldn't dress like a slob!" Dr. Goulston suggests that you give him some breathing room and say something indirect, for example:

> *I was thinking of how you dress like a slob and how it pisses me off. I put myself in your shoes, and this is what I came up with. You must feel so much pressure to be a good dad, a good husband, a good employee . . . you must feel that everyone is demanding that you behave a certain way. So maybe you're doing this stuff as a way of saying, "This is one thing in my life that belongs to me."*

If you approach your man in this way—"I realize that the world is making you feel like your head's going to explode, or

maybe *I'm* making you feel like your head's going to explode"—
then you're getting to the *real* conversation. Feeling acknowledged in this way, your man may slowly start to realize that he
can say "no" to you (and his other "masters") without feeling
guilty, and stop saying "no" through his sloppy appearance.

What if your man is self-destructive?

In some cases, your man's issues may be more serious than
untrimmed nose hairs or frayed clothes. For example, what if he's
so overweight that he's jeopardizing his health? What if he hasn't
exercised in years? What if he drinks *way* too much beer? And
what if he yells at you if you so much as bring up these subjects?

Dr. Goulston suggests that a man like this may be engaging
in self-destructive behavior as a coping mechanism. "If he has to
do very destructive things to cope, he may be coping with a lot
that you may not be aware of," he says.

Know what a shower is? "A shower, in addition to something
you have in your bathroom, is often a place where grown men
go to cry when they feel they can't keep their promise to their
wives and children that they could take care of them," says Dr.
Goulston. "But some men don't go to the shower. They go to
food and alcohol."

When the man you love isn't taking good care of himself, then
the way to his heart is through his fear. "Let him know that you
understand and that you don't think any less of him," suggests
Dr. Goulston. "Tell him, 'I realize that there are a lot of things
that are stressful and intimidating in your life. There are probably
times when you don't even know how you're going to keep doing
it. And the things that you do that seem unhealthy seem pref-
erable to not dealing with this stuff at all.' "

Get to the bottom of your man's self-destructive behavior. Be his ally, partner, and loving helpmate in this. If necessary—i.e., if you suspect that his problems are bigger than both of you— it's time to get some advice from a psychotherapist or your family doctor.

What do women want, anyway?

When I asked women the question "What makes a man look good?" I received a range of interesting responses:

Clothes and confidence are extremely important. Even if his body isn't the best, nice clothes and high self-esteem make up for that.

Health, confidence, body. Clothes are relatively unimportant.

A twinkle in his eye.

I can find a lot of quirky things attractive about a man—a well-placed scar, sexy neck, full lips, foreign accent, interesting sense of style. I think the most unattractive feature as a man gets older is the pot belly. Good clothes and charisma can really help a man's appearance.

A man should be well-groomed, but with an artistic, free-spirited flair.

Cleanliness. Dressing well with confidence.

Charisma, confidence, a sense of humor, vibrant health, and a nice body.

Health and confidence are very important things for me. Nice clothes make a difference—not necessarily expensive clothes, but a man who has put some thought into what he's wearing is definitely more attractive.

Pleasant mien—not too formal or preppy or schlumpy.

Confidence and a great sense of humor.

Vibrant health is most important.

A good body helps, but confidence and attitude can increase the attractiveness of a man.

Kindness, confidence, health, looks, nice body . . . in that order.

Good grooming, clean clothes, positive demeanor.

It would be possible to be good-looking on charisma alone.

Charisma and confidence. I think charisma makes all the difference.

I actually like men who don't put much thought into their looks. Although I think all men look great in suits.

Notice that not one of them replied *abs of steel . . . Rolex watches . . . Russell Crowe's bod.* When it comes to men's looks, the women I spoke to seemed most impressed by charisma, confidence, and health—followed by other considerations like style and an eye for clothes.

Of course, these qualities are often related. A man who has confidence and charisma may be inclined to dress well. A man who enjoys good health may also happen to be in good shape.

Women want their men to look good . . . but "looking good" can mean a lot of different things.

Furthermore, what women want . . . and what their men *think* they want . . . can be different, too.

Unconditionally yours

Barry, who is 50-ish, does not like the fact that a man has to "look good" for his woman. To him, it is a symbol of the frailties of human relationships.

"Unfortunately, at the bottom of this is a reason that is rather frightening but true," he says, "which is that love, much as we wish it were otherwise, is not unconditional for spouses, girlfriends, and boyfriends. We never really shed the obligation to perform for each other to some degree. We have to continually earn each other's admiration and love. It's not something that is just signed, sealed, and delivered with a ring or the joining of households."

We all want to be loved unconditionally. We all like to think that even if we gain 50 pounds, get disfiguring scars, or lose all our hair, our mates will still stand by us and love us for forever.

Keep this in mind when you're scrutinizing how your man looks and whether you should try to "make it better." Maybe he has a big belly. Maybe he wears rumpled shirts. Maybe he forgets to comb his hair. Maybe his shoes never match his outfits.

But how important are these things to you? Which ones have a negative enough effect on his health, his well-being, his success in life, or the success of your relationship that they're worth bringing up with him?

If your man is a lighthearted, good-humored kind of guy who doesn't mind constructive criticism about his appearance, then go for it.

But if he's not, try to remember how frail he is inside, and how frail he might perceive your love for him to be. Pick your battles, and proceed with caution.

Or maybe throw them all out the window and decide that your honey is just fine with his big belly, rumpled shirts, messy hair, and out-there shoes.

Chapter Two

"But that's the beauty of it, Rita! I don't have to worry about my fat intake today. I'm having a quadruple bypass tomorrow!"

Feeding Your Man

Melissa, 44, and Bob, 50, have been living together for five years. Melissa—who is in the health care profession—is deeply concerned about Bob's eating habits:

> He is out of shape and overweight. He eats lots of high-fat, low-quality food and gets mad if this is discussed. He does not like any low-fat cooking, although I certainly do it; he is convinced that anything low-fat is bad. I wish he were more aware of the health implications of being fat. I hate that his health is at such risk from his being overweight, but he can't get out of his own way to do something about it, even though not losing weight, not exercising, and not getting his blood pressure down are no doubt shortening his life.

Like Melissa, many women I spoke to were concerned about their man's eating habits. And with good reason: According to 1989–1994 figures collected by the Center for Disease Control's National Center for Health Statistics, 59.4 percent of men ages 20–72 were considered overweight. Of those men, 19.9 percent were considered obese. Both figures were up from previous years. Not surprisingly, men and women have their differences when it comes to gaining—and losing—weight. Have you ever noticed that you don't see a lot of men with big behinds? Have you ever noticed that you *do* see a lot of women with, um, that feature? We women tend to gain weight in our lower bodies. That means the thighs and buttocks, although the backs of our arms can be "fat magnets," too. Conversely, men tend to gain weight in their upper bodies—i.e., waist, chest, and stomach.

The upper-lower thing has various ramifications (other than making women look like pears and men like apples). Because lower-body fat is harder to lose than upper-body fat, it's more difficult for women to shed pounds than it is for men. (Sorry, ladies!) But while men can shed pounds more quickly than women, they can gain them more quickly, too.

And here's the *really* bad news: All that extra padding around their precious tickers puts men at increased risk for heart disease, diabetes, and other chronic illnesses.

There's no doubt about it. Your man's less-than-nutritious eating habits can seriously jeopardize his health. That's reason enough for you to be concerned.

Of course, there can be other compelling reasons as well. A poor diet can sap your man's energy and make him tired, fuzzy-brained, and cranky. (And who needs *that*?) It can set a bad example for the kids. (Dad can gorge on Twinkies, so why can't they?) It can make it harder for *you* to eat well. (Have you ever tried to lose weight when your mate insists on stocking the freezer with microwave pizzas and pints of Fudge Ripple?) It can mean having to spend major bucks on new, larger-size clothes for your man. ("My husband's gained weight, so I have to replace all his pants!" complained one woman.)

It can also have an undesirable effect on the desire factor.

"When he is in his heaviest periods, I am less sexually attracted to him," says Melissa of her overweight man, Bob.

This speaks directly to my point about everything being connected. If your man gains weight, you may find yourself less interested in being frisky with him. And less friskiness can mean less emotional intimacy and less overall satisfaction with the relationship. This, in turn, can contribute to your man's love affair with Doritos, his inability to fit into his old Levis, and his stubborn refusal to do anything about it.

Now we're back to why you don't feel like being frisky with him. And why there's all that pent-up (or not-so-pent-up) resentment: "Why won't you lose weight?" "Why won't you stop nagging me about it?" And on and on.

It's a vicious cycle. Fortunately, it's a cycle you can help put an end to.

Why is your man putting it on?

Gina, 33, has been married twice and is now single. She figures men "put it on" after marriage or moving in together because they don't need to impress you anymore.

"They start gaining weight, just because there is no need to hunt for someone," Gina theorizes. "They already have you—or so they think!"

There are many reasons why your man might be gaining weight—and in some cases, they are reasons that can apply to a woman as well:

• **Your man doesn't know when to stop eating.** "I think he eats more than he really has to," 25-year-old Lisa says of her 33-year-old boyfriend, Eric, whom she describes as being in good shape except for his "big belly." Many men (and women) are not attuned to their hunger/fullness signals, and continue munching away even after their tummies have had enough.

• **Your man eats too fast.** "He grew up in a family with lots of children and not enough food to go around, so he learned to shovel it in *fast*," says 33-year-old Maryann of her husband, Kevin. "He still does it at the dinner table, in front of the kids." It takes about 20 minutes for the "Okay, I'm full!" signal to travel from the stomach to the brain. If your man is a speed-eater, he's going to consume way more than he needs before he realizes he's had enough.

• **Your man likes big portions.** When it comes to food, size matters. "If a dish of ice cream is good, a gallon is better," says 50-year-old Barb about her 61-year-old husband, Mitch.

• **Your man thinks "dieting" is a woman thing.** Until the last few decades, it wasn't considered manly for men to dwell too much on their figures. Now, with the advent of magazines like *Men's Health* and all the guys in their 20s, 30s, and 40s (and beyond) hitting the gym, men are more aware of the importance of eating well and staying fit. However, your man may be one of those old-school hold-outs who thinks HDL is a new sports league, "low-fat" is a four-letter word, and the only reason for the existence of lettuce is to pile it onto a Quarter Pounder with extra cheese.

• **Your man isn't 18 anymore.** Shucks! I mean, the reality is, it becomes harder for men to take it off and keep it off as they get older. Over the years, their metabolism slows down, and their bad eating and drinking habits start to catch up with them. Stress is also a factor. As work pressures, money pressures, and all those other grown-up pressures pile up, they turn to food in order to "release."

• **Your man is in denial.** Some men just don't seem to realize that their beloved beer bellies may not be so attractive to women. They can also be operating under a double standard. One woman complained, "I work hard to be fit, and my boyfriend constantly praises me for my 'cute little body.' But when I suggest to him he could stand to lose a few pounds, he accuses me of being shallow!"

• **Your man is depressed.** Depression can lead to overeating (as well as the converse, a loss of appetite). Other signs of depression include fatigue, loss of energy, sleeping too little or too much, feelings of worthlessness, and loss of interest in his usual activities. If you suspect that your man may be suffering from depression, make an appointment for him to see your family physician ASAP.

• **You're overweight.** If you're overweight, it's going to be a *whole lot harder* to convince your man to be a lean, mean machine. You can't expect him to watch his fat and calorie intake if you're not going to practice what you preach.

The ABCs of feeding your man

Perhaps your man just needs to eat more fresh veggies. Or perhaps your man's idea of the four major food groups is donuts, hot dogs, cheese curls, and beer—and that's it. Whatever the case, how do you encourage him to eat better?

First and foremost, make it about more than the food.

"Create an atmosphere in your home in which health is a priority," says Jeanine Barone.

Barone is a nutritionist and exercise physiologist in New York

Does Age Matter?

Are younger men more appearance-conscience than older men? Some older men may be more fixed in their ways and harder to change than younger men. On the other hand, in one woman's words: "Aside from gay men and vain men and men who read *Men's Health*, men in their 20s are just as bad as men in their 60s. They eat crap, they hang out with their beer-guzzling buddies, and they watch *South Park*."
You be the judge.

City. She was once a guest on *The Late Show with David Letterman* to discuss how to lower his cholesterol level. She even brought him a tray of cholesterol-lowering oat-bran muffins she had baked for him to eat.

Says Barone, " 'Health' is about more than putting some greens on your man's dinner plate. It should go on all day long. It should be part of your relationship as a couple."

How do you make that happen? For starters, try the following suggestions:

(Note: Many of these suggestions presume that you'll be doing the lion's share of the cooking. I feel that this is necessary if you're going to take the lead in making your man healthier. Once the changes are in place, he will hopefully be able to return the favor and grill up some healthy gourmet meals for you. But even if you don't want to be Head Chef, the principles I discuss here should help you steer your man in the right direction.)

• **Do it gradually.** Don't make some sort of dramatic announcement like, "Honey, I've decided that this family is going to go low-fat!" *Uh-uhn*. The trick is to take baby steps, so that your man can get used to new tastes, new portions, and other healthy new habits at his own speed. In fact, don't even use words like *low-fat* and *diet* unless your man is already on board. Let him start feeling better, thinner, and more energetic—and then fill him in. Maybe.

• **Find your man's button—and work it.** Every man has a button. Does your man feel middle-aged and mortal? Slowly educate him about the diet-health connection and make him realize that eating better can often translate into living longer. Is sex really important to your guy? Tell him that you would have sex *a lot more often* if he'd join you in losing a few pounds. Then, with every pound he sheds, tell him how much his new body turns you on. Your man wants to look sexy for you!

• **Make it yummy.** "Prepare a nice, healthy meal that's well-flavored," recommends Barone. "Unless you have a tofu chunk hanging out there, men aren't going to notice the difference." Your man won't mind that you're serving new stuff if it tastes really, really good. Use spices and herbs creatively. Gourmet vinegars and bottled sauces, especially Asian ones, can add exotic flare to familiar foods without piling on calories and fat. For dinner, consider multiple courses: a low-fat soup (not cream-based!), followed by the main course, followed by a green salad, followed by a fruity dessert.

• **Be mindful of your food—and of each other.** One of the reasons your man eats way too much (and way too fast) is because he's doing something else at the same time. Watching *Seinfeld* reruns or catching up on back issues of *Sports Illustrated* over dinner will keep him from noticing his hunger/ fullness signals. It will also keep him from noticing just how good the food *tastes*, which can leave him feeling deprived later. Encourage him to sit down with you at the table without any other distractions. Light pretty candles; play soft jazz or classical music; set the table with nice place settings. Look into his eyes and actually have a conversation. Do all this even if you have children.

• **Make your man slow down!** If the previous suggestion doesn't stop your man from shoveling it in, see if he'll do the following with you: Take a bite, put down the fork, and drink a sip of water. Do this for the entire meal. Here's another good tip: Don't serve the entire meal all at once. Bring the soup; let him eat that; then take a few minutes before bringing out the main course. While you're doing all this, make sure to ask him so many questions about his day, his vehicle, or his favorite baseball team that he'll be forced to slow down even more.

• **Hydrate your man.** This one is really, really important: Make sure he drinks eight glasses of water a day! Minimum! Water is necessary to help digest food, flush out toxins, and perform all sorts of other good deeds. Also, thirst can often be mistaken for hunger, which means that a tall, cold one should be the first line of defense against overeating. To hydrate your man, bring him a fresh glass of ice water throughout the day. Leave it near him—on his desk, on his nightstand, on the coffee table as he's watching TV—and he's sure to reach for it (especially if you add a lemon slice or a goofy straw). Also, buy him a big, sporty-looking water bottle and fill it up every morning for him to take to work. He can also load up on juices and other healthy, nonsugary, noncaffeinated drinks to achieve his hydration goal. Sports drinks are fine, too, but your man shouldn't be drinking eight servings of the stuff per day because of the added sodium and other power ingredients. *(Note: Clear or light yellow urine is a sign of good hydration. Dark yellow urine means your man needs to drink more. You can* *tell him these things if you feel comfortable talking bathroom talk with him.)*

• **Serve meat as a side dish, not as the main course.** "My husband *insists* on having meat with every meal," complained one woman. I'm sure he's not the only one. And yet study after study has shown that a diet high in saturated fat is a no-no, and we all know that meat is chock-full of saturated fat. Plus, the latest research points to a link between a high-meat diet and prostate cancer. So if your man is strictly a meat-and-potatoes kind of guy, slowly wean him off by buying smaller (and leaner) cuts. Use creative seasonings and low-fat sauces so he'll focus on *taste* more than on *portion*. Fix lots of courses so he'll feel full and satisfied. Go from serving meat every day to every other day, and then to a couple of times a week; replace some of the meat dishes with poultry and fish entrées. If your man insists on steak, go for "eye of round," which is leaner than other cuts. If he insists on bacon, go for Canadian bacon, which has less fat than regular bacon.

• **Downgrade his portions—gradually.** If your man is used to consuming a huge, heaping plate of pasta for dinner, start reducing that amount slowly, a few noodles at a time. Ditto for other main dishes, side dishes, and desserts.

• **Get into grazing.** Eating lots of small meals throughout the day makes a lot more sense than a big breakfast, big lunch, and big dinner. When you have a free Saturday or Sunday together, experiment with the joys of grazing. Feed your man a yummy but nutritious breakfast (think freshly squeezed OJ and a bowl of oatmeal with fresh fruit, brown sugar, and 1% milk); enjoy a toasted whole-grain English muffin with marmalade for "elevensies"; pack a light picnic lunch and go on a hike; beat the late-afternoon munchies with a handful of nuts or some air-popped popcorn. Finish the day with a fresh green salad, a baked potato with nonfat sour cream or nonfat creamy dressing, and grilled or broiled fish topped with mango salsa (chop a mango, then mix with chopped scallions, chopped cilantro, grated ginger, lime juice, and brown sugar to taste).

• **Make his calories count.** "Don't splurge on dumb foods all day," advises Barone. According to the *American Journal of Clinical Nutrition*, American adults get one-third of their daily calorie intake from foods high in sugar, fat, and oil—but low in nutritional value. If your man is supposed to be consuming no more than 3,000 calories daily (this will depend on his age, height, fitness level, and fitness goals, if any), he can blow 25 percent of his quota *just like that* on two slices of frozen pizza. Does he really want the pizza *that much*? For the same number of calories, he could have had a yummy three-course meal.

• **Dispense health information in bite-size nuggets.** Don't bombard your man with the latest health findings—"I heard on *Oprah* this," "I read in *Time* magazine *that*"—hoping to scare him into giving up french fries, salami, Little Debbies, and whatever other weaknesses he may have. Your man is likely to tune you out with that all-too-common defense of, "Yeah, yeah, those doctors say one thing one day, and they say something else the next." Pick and choose your health sound bytes. A line like "I heard on CNN that men who eat a lot of meat are at greater risk for prostate cancer" is sure to get his attention. Let it sink in for a while—and in the meantime, see if he makes a peep when you start serving fewer burgers.

• **Let him watch.** Fifty-one-year-old Wendy changed the way she cooked to benefit herself first, and her husband second.

Fortunately, her husband caught on. "Just relax and put that energy into improving yourself," Wendy advises. "Teach by example." This is good advice, especially if your man is reluctant to change his eating habits, or if the two of you are "just dating" and you're not in a position to take control of his kitchen. Put the focus on you and *your* food selections. If your man sees how smartly you cook, shop, and order at a restaurant, he may pick up your cues and start doing some of that stuff himself. Don't give him a running commentary of your clever food choices, though; for example, "I *always* order the dressing on the side"; "I *never* use butter on my bread"; or "Two percent-*ugh*!" Just do your thing and be cool about it.

• **If necessary, use deception.** "I spent a year pouring regular half and half out of the carton and replacing it with no-fat half and half," one woman confessed. She eventually told her boyfriend, "and now *he* buys the no-fat half and half." Barone recommends the same tactic for milk: Gradually replace your man's whole milk with 2%, then 1%.

• **If necessary, get outside help.** If your man is seriously overweight, the first step should be an appointment with the family doctor. He or she will be able to advise your man on a course of action.

What your man hears when he hears the word *vegetarian*

"Men associate 'vegetarian' with boring, difficult, not filling, and not pleasant to eat," says Barone.

Wrong! Vegetarian dishes can be exciting, easy, filling, and

Grains Are Our Friends

Whole grains are rich in protein, complex carbs, vitamins, and minerals. They are also excellent sources of fiber (translation: good for regularity) and are low in fat. To add more grain to your man's diet, try:

- Couscous
- Polenta
- Tabbouleh
- Whole-wheat or cracked-rye cereals
- Millet (great side dish!)

If you're using prepackaged grain mixes—a lot of them will have an Italian or Near East theme—make sure to check the labels. They can be high in sodium. They can also be made from refined grains, which are not as desirable as whole grains.

completely pleasant—as long as they're prepared well and presented with panache.

Pick up some vegetarian cookbooks at the bookstore and try some recipes that look tasty to you. When you serve them to your man, don't announce: "Guess what, honey? *This is vegetarian!*" Let his taste buds be the judge.

Barone also suggests that a Gardenburger with low-fat cheese, tomato slices, relish, ketchup, and mustard is almost indistinguishable from the real thing. There's a challenge for you and your men, ladies—a blind burger taste test.

And if your man is fond of grilling, ask him to fire up some vegetables for you. Eggplant, zucchini, onions, mushrooms, corn on the cob, and peppers are wonderful on the grill. Try a marinade made with low-sodium soy sauce, grated ginger, garlic, and lemon or orange juice. Or brush the veggies with a little olive oil and fresh herbs. Serve with couscous and a green salad, and your man will have an exciting, easy, filling, and completely pleasant meal.

Hold the Cheese, Please

According to a report from the Center for Science in the Public Interest, cheese is the number-one source of saturated fat in the American diet. As we all know, saturated fat is the stuff that clogs your arteries. If your man is a cheese-lover, opt for lower-fat options like feta cheese and cheeses made from skim milk.

How to feed your man when he's on his own

"I have no influence over his food when I'm not there," says Barb, 50, of her 61-year-old husband, Mitch. "I'd see his car after a business trip and he'd have empty Dunkin' Donuts boxes, soda cans, and Quarter Pounder wrappers."

"He eats popcorn for dinner if I'm not there," says Susana, 44, of husband, Frank, who's 56.

Lisa, 25, has a similar complaint about her 33-year-old boyfriend, Eric. "He eats well when we're together, it's just when he's alone."

It's hard to have an influence on your man's diet when he's at work, on the road, out with his friends, or home alone. When you're together, you can make healthy meals and snacks for him, but when you're apart, it's Danishes on the run . . . three-martini lunches with clients . . . beers and nachos with his buds after hours.

Hopefully, all the tweaking and talking you do with your man about eating well in general will eventually sink in—and inspire him to make better food choices when he's not with you. There comes a moment for many of us when we stare at a plate of greasy fries or a massive piece of chocolate cake and think: *Is it worth it? Do I really want this? I spent an hour on the treadmill today—do I want to blow that?*

Until that moment comes for your man, here are some ways to feed him when he's on his own:

• **Pack his snacks.** Send him to work with baggies of fresh berries and grapes. If a donut or Danish is part of his morning-commute routine, pack him a bagel with strawberry or raspberry jam. Include cute and/or naughty little love notes.

• **Pack his lunches.** Give him lots of courses. Make them healthy but incredibly tasty. A sample lunch: tuna salad (made with low- or nonfat mayo and lots of relish) on whole-grain bread, a small bag of pretzels, fresh strawberries with nonfat chocolate dip, and a bottle of mineral water. Or instead of tuna salad, you could make your man a sandwich with fresh turkey breast or skinless chicken, vine-ripened tomato slices, greens, and nonfat salad dressing. Other lunch ideas include pita bread, fresh veggies, and hummus, or last night's yummy leftovers.

• **Buy him a mini-fridge for his office.** Stock it with nonfat yogurt, fruit, and bottled waters and juices.

• **Freeze a couple of dinners for him if you're going to be away.** Or buy him some healthy frozen dinners. Barone recommends vegetarian frozen dinners made by Cedar Lane (they're low-fat) and vegan frozen dinners made by Mon Cuisine (also low-fat). If your man requires some meat or seafood with his microwaveable chow, you might try the following frozen dinners, recommended by the guys at *Men's Health* magazine in their December 2000 issue: Lean Cuisine Café Classics Shrimp and Angel Hair Pasta, Uncle Ben's Teriyaki Chicken Rice Bowl, Stouffer's Hearty Portions Beef Pot Roast with

Roasted Peppers and Green Beans, and Healthy Choice Beef Tips Portobello.

How to feed your man when you're out on the town

We all do it. When we're at a restaurant, we feel like we can "treat ourselves." We have a couple of cocktails to start. We load up on the bread and butter. We order an appetizer that's probably as big as an entrée should be. *Then* there's the entrée. All along, the wine's been flowing. And of course, there's dessert and maybe even an after-dinner drink.

Putting on your little black dress and having your man take you to a romantic candlelit bistro is one of the great pleasures in life. Unfortunately, it's easy to let healthy habits slip when there are tempting menu items involved.

With that in mind, here are some tips on living it up while keeping it lite:

• Barone favors high-end Thai, Vietnamese, Korean, Malaysian, Indian, and other Asian restaurants. She cites the nice atmosphere, exotic preparations and spices, and numerous low-fat and healthy options.

• Restaurant portions are usually *way* bigger than they need to be. Suggest to your man that you order two salads (dressing on the side) and two appetizers, then sit very close together and share everything. Afterward, share a small but decadent dessert.

• Pass on the bread basket. If your man insists on having bread, encourage him to skip those deceptively eency-weency containers of butter.

• Soup is very filling. Suggest to your man that the two of you have a soup course before the entrée. (Just make sure it's not cream-based.)

• Pasta is a terrific choice as long as it's not slathered with a cream sauce. If your man orders the Fettucine Alfredo, lobby for the marinara instead. Also beware of portions. According to the *Tufts University Health and Nutrition Letter*, a pasta dish at an Italian restaurant might include eight (!) one-cup servings.

• Steer your man toward broiled fish or chicken—no deep-fried stuff, no rich sauces.

• Ply your man with ice water, which is not only healthy but filling.

• Make sure your man takes it easy with the liquor. Not only is getting sloshed bad for the obvious reasons, but it can also impair his ordering abilities ("Gimme another round of those little stuffed potato thingies, will ya?") and mess with his hunger/fullness signals.

Good food, bad food

In this day and age, with scientists and other experts bombarding us with nutrition updates—"eat this, don't eat that"— it's hard to keep track of what's healthy and what's not. Hopefully, this book will help make things a little simpler. In addition

The Way to a Man's Heart . . . and Other Parts of Him, Too

If you're familiar with *Like Water for Chocolate* (the book or the film), you know about the primal connection between eating and sexual passion. In addition to chocolate, other seductive foods include oysters and strawberries. For a wonderful lineup of lust-inducing recipes, check out *Intercourses: An Aphrodisiac Cookbook* by Martha Hopkins and Randall Lockridge.

to the foods I mentioned above, here are some others your man should eat more of:

• **Garlic.** It's been known to keep Dracula at bay, but did you know that it may also reduce the risk of heart attack, lower cholesterol levels, protect against certain kinds of cancer, and even help fight the common cold, flu, sinusitis, and bronchitis? Increase your man's garlic intake by throwing it into salads, soups, stews, pastas, and marinades. Brush a piece of lightly toasted bread with olive oil and a crushed clove of garlic. Note: Garlic's cancer-fighting chemical can decompose on heating. If you intend to cook it, let it first sit for 10 minutes after chopping. This will result in a groovy chain reaction that will boost levels of the cancer-fighting substance.

• **Fruits and vegetables.** Well, duh. Still, you probably didn't realize that fruits and veggies can deliver more than just vitamins and fiber. Prunes, raisins, blueberries, blackberries, strawberries, raspberries, and plums are serious cancer-fighters; so are kale and spinach. And you've heard the phrase "an apple a day keeps the doctor away"? Recent studies show that eating apples can also reduce the risk for certain cancers, heart attacks, and strokes, and can also boost lung function. Tomatoes, watermelon, and pink grapefruit are good sources of lycopene, which may help to prevent prostate cancer—a big concern for guys. In general, fresh fruits and veggies are usually best; if you opt for frozen or canned, check labels carefully for high sodium and fat content. Some exceptions to the "fresh is best" rule are carrots and tomatoes; cooking and processing increase the beta carotene in carrots and the lycopene in tomatoes.

Here are some foods your man should try to avoid:

• **Salt.** An estimated 80 percent of Americans consume at least 10 times as much sodium as they need. And too much salt has been linked to a host of health problems, including high blood pressure and heart disease. Season your man's food with herbs and spices instead. Learn to read labels—there is an appalling amount of sodium in many packaged foods.

• **Trans fats.** When it comes to heart health, some experts consider trans fats more lethal than animal fat. Trans fats—which are found in stick margarine, solid vegetable shortening, foods fried in hydrogenated fat, and favorite goodies such as cookies, cakes, and potato chips—have also been linked to cancer and diabetes. To avoid trans fats, opt for trans-fat-free margarines (such as Promise) or very small amounts of butter. Also steer clear of deep-fried foods and packaged foods that include "partially hydrogenated oils" in the ingredients.

• **HAAs.** Huh? Those initials stand for "heterocyclic aromatic amines," which are formed when meat is cooked at high temperatures (for example, when you pan-fry burgers). The problem is, these HAAs can cause cancer. If your man's gotta have his burgers, be sure to microwave the patties for one to three minutes first. Then pour off the liquid and pan-fry.

Your man's sweet tooth

Speaking of "bad food" . . . a number of women complained about their men's weakness for desserts and sugary snacks:

I'd like him to eat fewer sweets.

He eats way too many sweets.

I'm a failure getting him to cut back on peanut butter M&Ms and Mrs. Smith's pumpkin pie.

He will have a hot fudge sundae whenever there is one available. If I buy ice cream for our grandchildren, he will finish everything up.

There's nothing wrong with a sweetie here and there. "We eat something because it tastes good," Barone points out. "And sweets taste good."

The key is moderation . . . and awareness. Try to make your man aware of his dessert options. He could have that slice of stale, barely edible apple pie from the deli. But for the same number of calories, he could have a bowl of Häagen-Dazs chocolate sorbet each night *for the next four nights*. (Plus, the sorbet has zero fat in it.)

The other key, of course, is stealth. Tonight, substitute nonfat frozen yogurt or ice cream for the fatty stuff; top with strawberry and banana slices, nonfat chocolate sauce, and nonfat whipped topping; and share with two spoons. See if he notices.

Chapter Three

"I tell ya, Helen, I rue the day that I signed us up for those Riverdance lessons."

Exercising Your Man

When it comes to looking and feeling good, one of the most important things your man can do is to exercise regularly. But many women—including 31-year-old Darlene—can't seem to get their men moving:

Marc was thin as a rail when we met in college. He was on the cross-country skiing team, and he played a lot of tennis, too. He always seemed to burn off whatever he ate.

After college, we got married. We have three kids now, and Marc works long, crazy hours at the insurance company. I don't know the last time he exercised. His pants don't fit anymore, and sometimes he gets out of breath playing with the kids in the yard.

I tried to get him to go to the gym with me on weekends—they have free day care there for the kids—but he said weekends are the only time he has to do stuff around the house. I bought him a treadmill for Christmas last year, but he never uses it.

I don't know what to do to try to get him back into shape. It's not like I want him to be super-skinny again like he was in college. I just want him to be healthier and more energetic.

Health and *energy* are two key reasons why your man should be putting on the running shoes, dusting off the rowing machine, or brushing up on his backstroke. Regular exercise can help your man reduce the risk for cardiovascular disease, coronary heart disease, high blood pressure, colon cancer, osteoarthritis, and more. It can help relieve stress. It can improve mood and vitality.

Oh . . . and if that's not enough to convince your man: According to a University of California study, guys who exercise three times a week have three times more sex than guys who don't. Hmmm.

Bottom line: Exercise can help your man look better, feel better, and live longer. *And* have more sex.

But despite these boffo benefits, your man may still be reluctant to incorporate a regular exercise routine into his schedule. Here are some possible explanations:

- He is not aware of the benefits of exercising—or the downsides of *not* exercising.

- He feels as though he doesn't have time.

- He doesn't know how to get started.

- He began an exercise program once or twice that didn't work out for him, so he just gave up.

- He doesn't like gyms or classes.

- His friends don't exercise.

- He doesn't want to compete with younger guys or guys who may be more fit.

- He has "bad knees" or some other physical problem that makes him think he can't exercise.

- He equates being out of shape with growing older, so it's "okay" not to exercise.

- He doesn't want to disappoint himself—or you—by starting a exercise program and then failing.

Like eating well, exercise is something you can't force your man to do. He has to want to do it for himself. If you're lucky, he may get motivated on his own—by reading an article about weight-training, by wanting to fit into his favorite suit again, or by having a milestone birthday. He may get motivated by co-workers who go to the gym at lunch or play racquetball together. He may get motivated by your four-year-old, who grabs him around the middle and screeches "Daddy's big belly! Daddy's big belly!"

But if these motivations aren't there—or if your man needs an extra nudge—there are many ways you can encourage him to get up and get moving.

Why your man doesn't want to go to the gym

"A lot of guys aren't comfortable going to the gym because they don't like looking at the muscleheads," says Regina Cornell.

Cornell is a personal trainer in Saratoga Springs, New York. She says that a lot of her male clients are average, everyday guys. They seem to like working with her because she's a slim, petite woman and not some huge iron man they have to compete against.

Noah Pacifico, director of Sales and Marketing at World Gyms of New York City, agrees. "When a man is not in the shape he

Short Workouts Count, Too

According to a recent study, men who burned 1,000 to 2,000 calories a week through exercise had 20 percent lower risk for heart disease than men who exercised less—regardless of whether the exercise was done during several long sessions or a number of short ones. The average age of the men in the study was 66.

wants to be in, he's afraid that the gym is going to be full of big guys, and that he's going to be out of place. But it's not like that."

Pacifico says that at World Gyms, they put the emphasis on fun. "We try to tell the guys it's not a place to lose weight. It's a place to have *fun*."

Pacifico explains that they try to get men who may be new to exercise into different programs like yoga, beginning boxing, and resistance training. And it's all about quality, not quantity. "Three days a week is enough. We just want them to get their feet wet."

Pacifico sees a lot of women getting gift memberships for their husbands and boyfriends, and vice versa.

As for the men, he finds it rewarding to see them "getting into it." "It's like in the beginning, these guys are saying, 'Jeez, my wife wants me to join the gym, what's she trying to tell me?' And then they come in and they realize, 'Hey, this isn't so bad. This is fun!' "

Still, some men may prefer the privacy and flexibility of working out at home. Or they may find a gym environment too "artificial" and prefer outdoor activities like hiking, rock-climbing, or cycling. Or there may not be a gym that's close to home or work. Or they might not want to spring for the cost of a membership.

However, if you think your man might be interested in joining a gym—and just needs some extra encouragement—then go for it. Most gyms offer a day-use or trial rate. Get him to go with you one afternoon so the two of you can try it out together. If necessary, make it about *you*: "Honey, I'm feeling flabby, and I'm thinking about joining a gym. Will you go to the Y with me and help me check it out?"

And there's always that gift membership. "For my husband's birthday, I got him a three-month gym membership, so he wouldn't feel pressured to do it for a whole year," said 26-year-old Karen. "I also got him a gift certificate for workout clothes and shoes. He was really into it."

Note: If your man is over 40 and he's been sedentary for a while—or if he's *any* age and has medical issues such as a heart condition—make sure he gets a physical exam before embarking on an exercise program. And another note: Muscle weighs more than fat. If your man complains because he's been working out for a month only to gain five pounds, remind him of this very important fact. The true test should be how his body looks and how his clothes are fitting him.

Sweaty stuff for you to do together

Twenty-five-year-old Lisa has gotten her 33-year-old boyfriend, Eric, to start jogging with her. "We've run a bit together, although getting him to go on his own is a trial. He is receptive, though, and always feels good when we're done."

"I exercise a lot, which means that my boyfriend ends up exercising a lot by default," says Kyra, who is in her 40s. "If he wants to see me on a Sunday afternoon and I happen to be going

Use It or Lose It

Unless your man is a professional athlete, he can probably skip his workouts for a couple of weeks without experiencing a serious decline in aerobic capacity. Longer than that, though, and he will probably need to jump-start his program at a slightly lower level, then gradually build back.

mountain-climbing, he'll come along just so he can spend time with me."

If you're like Lisa, you could encourage your man to join you in a regular program of exercise.

Or if you're like Kyra, you could exercise on your own, for *you*—and then invite your man to join in if and when he wants.

Either way, the emphasis should be on being active and having fun—not on making your man feel as though he has to drop 10 pounds or develop rock-hard biceps by next Tuesday.

To get you started, here is a list of activities you could do together:

• Take walks. Get in the habit of taking a brisk walk together every night after dinner. If you have kids, bring them with you—even if it's just for a short walk.

• Join the gym together. Tell him how cute he looks in his shorts. Spot each other in the weight room. Towel each other off afterward.

• Hire a personal trainer for couple's sessions. Two of Cornell's favorite clients are a married couple in their 70s, whom she visits at home twice a month. An added benefit: It's usually cheaper for two people to sign up for a personal-training session together than for them to do it apart.

• Sign up for a coed yoga class. (For more on partner yoga, which is more specific to couples, see page 141.)

• Have a semi-weekly tennis date. All that "love" and "deuce" talk can be so inspiring!

• Go Rollerblading. Don't forget the helmets and pads!

• Go on hikes. Think nature hikes, urban hikes, and suburban hikes.

• Sign up for ballroom-dancing classes. If Argentinian Tango lessons are involved, *definitely* sign up. I guarantee you that it will do more for your sex life than Victoria's Secret and Viagra combined.

• Play racquetball, handball, or squash.

• If it's winter, take up skating, snow-shoeing, or cross-country skiing. Or take turns pulling each other around on a sled, like when you were kids.

• Set up a badminton net in the backyard.

• Sign up for a 5K charity race together. Spend the next few months training for it.

• Buy some used mountain bikes and helmets and go on long bike rides together. Explore the countryside or unknown neighborhoods. Pack healthy snacks and have a romantic picnic together.

• Plan an active trip for your next vacation. You could go trekking through Tuscany, snorkeling in the Keys, or exploring

A Home Gym on a Budget

For a few hundred bucks, you can purchase a basic home gym for your man (and yourself!). You'll need a flat/incline/decline bench, a barbell, about a hundred pounds of weights, and a jump rope. To cut costs even further, check out yard sales, used sporting goods stores, and want ads. Also try Internet shopping at sites like newyorkbarbells.com and fitnessfactory.com.

Mayan ruins in Guatemala. Spend the next few months getting in shape for it together.

• Do laps together a few times a week. Find a pool in your area—or better yet, a lake or an ocean beach. (If it's a beach, you can find a secluded spot afterward and pretend you're Burt Lancaster and Deborah Kerr in *From Here to Eternity*.)

Sweaty stuff for him to do without you

Some couples don't like to exercise together. Your exercise is your thing . . . his exercise is his thing . . . and never the twain shall meet.

But what if you have a fitness routine going and your man doesn't? *Then* what? Your job is to get him interested in doing *something*.

Of course, your man is like you. If he likes a particular kind of exercise, he'll probably do it—and keep doing it. But if he doesn't, he won't.

"Find the fit," recommends Cornell.

She finds that her male clients tend to like playing sports, such as basketball or tennis. They also like to lift weights and run, either outside or on a treadmill.

Here are some ideas for workouts your man might enjoy:

• **Strength-training.** This consists of lifting weights, doing calisthenics (such as ab crunches and tricep dips), and otherwise working on the major muscle groups. Your man can do this at home or at the gym. (Note: Once your man hits his 30s, he should ideally be splitting his time between strength-training, which works muscles, and aerobic exercise, which works the heart.)

• **The Type-A Workout.** The Equinox Gym in New York City offers this new workout for busy, busy people. It's designed to cram an hour and 15 minutes of aerobics, strength-training, and other exercises into 40 intense minutes. If your man fits the profile, call your local gym and see if they offer something similar.

• **The SuperSlow Workout.** On the flip side, Ken Hutchins, founder of the SuperSlow Exercise Guild, believes in doing really, really slow reps on weight machines—and that's it. No aerobics whatsoever. He also believes in doing this workout only once a week to achieve maximum benefits. To get more information, check out his website at www.superslow.com.

• **Power walking.** Your man should aim to walk briskly for at least 30 minutes daily, or for an hour three or four times a week. He should pump his arms to work his upper body; he can opt to use small hand weights or not. Walking up and down hills and varying his terrain (grass, gravel, sand) can help build strength and stamina.

Working Out on a Business Trip

The next time your man goes on a business trip, pack some shorts, T-shirts, athletic socks, and running shoes in his bag—plus a jump rope. This way, if his hotel doesn't have a gym, he can use the jump rope in his room. He can also add jumping jacks, push-ups, ab crunches, and tricep dips (off a chair).

Still, it's probably not going to be too cool for you to announce to your man: "Honey, I just signed you up for the strength-training class at the gym!" The idea—and the impetus—have to come from him.

With that in mind, here are some tips for getting him started on a workout regimen of his own:

• **Leave fitness information lying around the house.** Get class schedules, gym membership forms, and sign-up sheets for athletic leagues and events. Pile them carelessly in a spot that is "yours" but where he's likely to see them. If he mentions them, act very blasé: "What? Oh, *that*. I don't know, I was thinking about maybe doing something."

• **Mention it once . . . maybe twice . . . and then drop it.** Say, "My friend Jim has a Tuesday night men's doubles thing, and some guy's dropping out, so they need a fourth. He thought you might be interested." If he *is* interested, he'll act on it. If he's not, don't harangue him.

• **Let it be his.** If your man *does* get into a regular exercise routine, whether it's jogging, Rollerblading, or kick-boxing, that's great news! Now your job is to step back and just be supportive. Let him have the time he needs to work out. After

Do Energy Bars Really Give You Energy?

Most energy bars will give your man energy because they contain boffo protein and calories. But many of them are packed with sugar (a.k.a. "high-fructose corn syrup," "cane syrup," and "maltodextrin"). Some can also be high in fat. Your man may be better off fueling himself with fruit, trail mix, a handful of nuts, or a sandwich. But if he likes the taste and convenience of energy bars, look for ones that are low in fat and sweetened with evaporated cane juice.

a few weeks, praise his efforts by telling him how sexy he's looking and how much you admire his discipline. But don't try to butt in with comments like, "Why did you skip your run today?" or "Don't you think *Intermediate* Kick-Boxing would be better for you?" Just let him do his thing.

Oh, you mean *that* kind of six-pack

If your man is interested in developing a "six-pack" (a.k.a. washboard abs), he's going to have to employ a multi-part strategy.

First, he's gotta do a lot of crunches. That's crunches, not sit-ups. Experts now recommend the former as the best kind of ab exercise.

To do a proper crunch, have your man lie on a mat or rug with his back flat, his knees bent, and his hands lightly supporting the back of his head or neck. Keeping his eyes focused on the ceiling, he should lift his shoulder blades off the floor . . . breathe out . . . lower them . . . breathe in. With each crunch, he should imagine his belly button kind of caving in toward the floor. He could start with three sets of 12 reps. (In plain English, that's 12 crunches, then a break, then 12 more, then a break, then 12 more.)

But crunches are not enough—i.e., they will not get rid of fat. If your man has a big belly and/or love handles, he'll have to lose them through aerobic exercise (such as jogging). Otherwise, the muscle tone he develops via the crunches will be hidden by layers of fat.

Oh, and don't forget . . . he should probably start cutting down on the *other* kind of six-packs.

Chapter Four

Surgeons at Wilton Medical Center prepare
for the world's first beer-bellyectomy.

Keeping Your Man Healthy

When it comes to her husband, Alan, Clara, 52, doesn't care too much about designer clothes or expensive haircuts. She does, however, care about his less-than-stellar health:

His dad died of a heart attack when he was in his 50s, and so did his dad. But Alan's in denial about all that. He won't lose the weight, and I can't get him to go in for his check-ups. I worry that he's not going to go to the doctor until it's too late.

When it comes to their men, most women would undoubtedly choose "good health" above good wardrobe, good biceps, good just about everything else. Health is the crucial foundation for living a long, active, happy life.

Of course, it also happens to be the crucial foundation for looking good. If your man isn't healthy, all the fancy suits and expensive grooming products in the world aren't going to make him look vibrant. If he *is* healthy, the sparkle in his eyes and the confidence in his step will reflect that.

"There's no question that if a man's health is good, he *feels* good, and that tends to make him *look* good," says Dr. Ken Goldberg.

Dr. Goldberg is the author of *When the Man You Love Won't Take Care of His Health.* He is also the medical director of the Male Health Institute in Dallas, Texas.

He agrees that just as good health tends to equal good appearance, poor health tends to equal poor appearance. In his words: "It's a vicious circle."

There are also illnesses and conditions that can directly affect the way your man looks. Dr. Goldberg cites rosacea (think Bill Clinton), acne, allergies, thyroid disease, and Grave's disease as a few examples. Side effects from medications can also impact your man's appearance.

If your man is suffering from *any* illness or condition that might be affecting his looks, his mood, his energy level, or his overall health, it's important to get him to the doctor.

Of course, that may not be as easy as it sounds.

Why your man hates going to the doctor

In his book, Dr. Goldberg writes: "Most men don't get themselves to the doctor when they should. Each year men visit the doctor 130 million fewer times than women do (even after adjusting the numbers so that prenatal care doesn't skew the results), and 37 million men haven't seen a doctor in the last two years."

He lists several common reasons why men drag their feet about visiting the doctor:

- They're afraid.

- They're embarrassed.

- It's a threat to their masculinity.

- They think they're invincible.

- It represents a loss of control.

Sound familiar?

Fortunately, you don't just have to sit back and do nothing while your man ignores his health and his doctor. For starters, try these strategies:

• **Become an authority on male health.** According to Dr. Goldberg, the first step you should take to help your man stay healthy is to educate yourself about men's health issues. Read books. Check out websites. Subscribe to health and wellness magazines and newsletters.

• **Get into his head.** If your man is suffering from digestive problems, chest pains, or other symptoms, he's likely to keep the information to himself and "tough it out." Understanding how your man's mind works when it comes to his health will make it easier for you to tell when he's not well—and figure out what to do about it.

• **Educate him—carefully.** Once you've become knowledgeable about male health, drop little nuggets of information here and there. If he complains about a symptom ("My knees hurt when I run," "I've been getting headaches at work"), give him an article about possible causes and let him do some detective work on the subject. (Guys *love* that.)

• **Do it together.** Go to the doctor with him. In preparing for his appointments, draft a list of questions for the doctor together along with your man's medical history. If he has a medical issue such as impotence, infertility, or heart disease, commit to working on a solution together.

• **Let him own the process.** Don't act like his mommy nagging him to go to the doctor or eat his broccoli. Let him feel like *he's* in charge of getting healthier and more health-savvy. Says Dr. Goldberg in his book, "Instead of reminding him that he should be going to the doctor, get out your date book and ask him when he'll be seeing the doctor so you can plan your schedule around it." Another tip: Ask him to take the kids to the doctor, which will help him become more familiar with health and medical issues. Also ask him to accompany you on *your* check-ups and doctor visits.

• **Work the male-bonding thing.** Men often prefer to get health advice from other men—even male strangers—than from their own wives and girlfriends. Encourage your man to find support groups, attend talks and seminars on cholesterol and other health topics, or just hang out at the gym, where "locker room talk" can often consist of "Yo, Mike, you ever get that pain in your lower back when you do crunches?"

• **Talk health with him.** Discuss interesting health news with him at the dinner table or while you're taking a walk together. ("Hey, I read this thing about high blood pressure in the paper today. . . .") The more health talk there is in his day-to-day life, the more it'll filter into his consciousness. Plus, the more familiar he is with health issues in general, the more comfortable he'll become with the topic of his *own* health—and the better he'll be at identifying any health problems in the future.

To Help Your Man Battle Cold and Flu Germs—Have More Sex with Him

Researchers at Wilkes University in Pennsylvania have discovered that having sex can boost levels of the cold- and flu-fighting antigen called immunoglobulin A, which means that you can have more fun *and* save money on antihistamines.

How often should your man go in for a routine check-up?

The answer to this question will depend a great deal on your man's family history (as well as his own medical history). His doctor will need to know *all the facts* before recommending a schedule of routine check-ups for your man.

Aside from the family and personal history factor, Dr. Goldberg recommends the following schedule for most men:

- Twice in their 20s

- Three times in their 30s

- Every other year in their 40s

- Once a year in their 50s and beyond

What about tests and vaccines and stuff like that?

Again, your man's doctor will be the best judge of how often your man should be getting various tests, screening procedures, and immunizations, but generally speaking, here is an approximate timetable:

• In his 20s and 30s, your man should be getting his blood pressure checked every two years, getting a professional skin exam every three years, and getting his cholesterol and HDL levels checked every five years. He should get a tetanus booster—which is actually a combination tetanus and diphtheria shot—every 10 years. If he is at risk for Hepatitis B, he should get a one-time Hepatitis B vaccine.

• Once your man hits his 40s, add to the above a fasting plasma glucose test every three years (to screen for diabetes). He should also increase the professional skin exam to yearly.

• Once your man hits his 50s, add to the above a fecal occult blood test every year, a digital rectal exam every year (to screen for prostate cancer), a prostate specific antigen (PSA) test every year, and colorectal cancer tests every 5 to 10 years.

• Regardless of your man's age, he should be performing a testicular self-exam and skin self-exam monthly. He should also go in for regular eye exams, depending on his eyesight and other eye-related issues.

• Once your man hits 65, he should do all of the above plus increase the cholesterol and HDL tests to every three to five years and the eye exam to every one to two years. He should also get a flu vaccine yearly as well as a one-time pneumococcal vaccine.

• If you or your man have other sexual partners, you should both be checked regularly for HIV. (And needless to say, you should both be using condoms every time you have sex.)

What to expect as your man gets older

Your man's body goes through a lot of wear and tear and use and abuse over the course of his lifetime. The result can be the so-called "degenerative diseases" of old age such as arthritis and heart disease.

But your man's body will also experience a number of changes that are part of the normal aging process. For example:

Stuff that will slow down or decrease:

- Metabolism

- Muscle strength (after he hits his mid-30s)

- Kidney function (after 40)

- Lean weight (in his 60s and 70s)

- Red blood cells (after he hits his mid-60s)

- Muscle mass (30 percent loss by the time he hits his 80s)

- Cartilage elasticity

- Height

- Heart rate

- Respiratory function

- His stomach's ability to empty

- Intestinal motility

- Glucose tolerance

Stuff that will speed up or increase:

- Chest circumference

- Total body weight (up to his late 50s)

- Stiffness of blood vessels and heart muscle

- Stomach acid

As your man gets older—and by "older," I mean in his 30s and beyond—learn to distinguish these normal signs of aging from symptoms that may indicate an underlying illness or condition. Illnesses and conditions to watch out for include (but are not limited to!) the following:

- Hypertension

- Stroke

- Heart disease

- Diabetes

- Arthritis

- Back problems

- Knee problems

- Alzheimer's disease

- Cancer

- Prostatitis

- Depression

Does Your Man Suffer from Low Testosterone?

According to some estimates, over four million American men—including men in their 30s and 40s—have lower-than-normal levels of testosterone. Symptoms include decreased sexual desire, impaired sexual performance, depression, lethargy, and loss of muscle mass in the upper body. If you suspect that your man may be suffering from a low testosterone count, have him checked by your family doctor. There are injections, pills, and other remedies available.

- Changes in sexual function

- Cataracts, glaucoma, and other vision problems

- Hearing problems

Invest in a good book on men's health or a general guide to family health and bone up on these and other illnesses and conditions. Become familiar with user-friendly medical websites such as Webmd.com, Mayoclinic.com, and Drkoop.com. And of course, if something seems to be ailing your man, call your physician and make an appointment—pronto.

Help your man say no to cigarettes

Beatrice, 49, can't get her husband, Chuck, to stop smoking cigarettes:

He's been smoking since he was in high school. He goes through about a pack a day. They stain his teeth. They make his hair and his skin and his clothes smell disgusting. They make him cough, and he doesn't exercise. I've asked him a million times to stop, but he won't, even though he knows it comes between us, plus it's going to kill him someday.

Smoking is *not healthy*. We all know this, right? Each cigarette shortens a person's life span by about 12 minutes. About 40 percent of all male cancers can be attributed to tobacco. When we're talking specifically lung cancer, the number jumps to a whopping 90 percent. Smoking has also been linked to impotence (because of blocked arteries), infertility, heart disease, emphysema, allergies, and gum disease. Then there are all the frightening statistics about what secondhand smoke can do to smokers' spouses, significant others, and worst of all, children.

If your man doesn't smoke, don't let him start! But if he *does* smoke, quitting is one of the most important things—if not *the* most important thing—he can do for his health. Here are some ways you can help as well as some facts to keep in mind:

• **Smoking is an addiction.** If your man refuses to quit, realize that he's not necessarily being stubborn or stupid. He's probably addicted to the stuff, both physically and psychologically. Think of nicotine addiction the same way you would think about drug addiction or alcohol addiction. Be fully aware of how powerful those little white sticks can be.

• **It has to be his decision.** As with other types of addiction, the choice to quit has to come from him. Of course, you can try to convince him by telling him all the reasons he should quit:

  ▪ He will live a longer, healthier life. (Cite cancer, heart disease, and all the other smoking-related illnesses mentioned above.)

- You and your kids will live longer, healthier lives without all that secondhand smoke in the house.
- His kisses will taste better.
- His clothes will smell nicer.
- He will save money in doctor bills and insurance premiums, not to mention the cost of the cigarettes themselves, which is tremendous.
- He will be able to play softball with your kids without huffing and puffing.
- He will set a good example for your kids, who are going to have to make the choice—to smoke or not to smoke?—when they're old enough to buy cigarettes (or old enough to bum from kids who are).
- He won't have to walk around with an oxygen tank strapped to his back when he's 65 years old.

• **Prepare for the big day.** Once your man makes the decision to quit, help him pick The Day—maybe his birthday, maybe your child's birthday, maybe your wedding anniversary, maybe the day you met. If no significant dates are on the horizon, just shoot for a specific day that's close, such as "next Monday" or "the first of the month." Encourage your man to make a list of the reasons he's quitting, to reinforce this wonderful, healthy step he's taking in his life. Also encourage him to tell other family members, friends, and co-workers about his decision so he can get lots of support and positive feedback.

• **Find a method that works.** One method that has been effective for many smokers is "nicotine replacement therapy": nicotine patches, nicotine gums, nicotine nasal sprays, or nicotine inhalers. These products work by delivering smaller and smaller doses of nicotine into the system over time and gradually weaning the person entirely. Other smoking-cessation strategies might include Zyban (a prescription antidepressant that reduces symptoms of nicotine withdrawal), hypnosis, acupuncture, going to Nicotine Anonymous meetings, or signing up for a stop-smoking class. Your family physician may be able to help as well—encourage your man to make an appointment. And keep in mind that "cold turkey" doesn't seem to work for many smokers.

• **Eliminate all traces of the past.** With your man's okay, throw out anything smoking-related in your house: lighters, matches, ashtrays, souvenirs with cigarette logos, and of course, the cigarettes themselves. Make an appointment with your man's dentist to have his tobacco-stained teeth polished so they're pearly white again. Send out all his yucky, smoky clothes to be professionally cleaned.

• **Stock up on substitutes.** On your man's Quit Day and beyond, make sure he has plenty of hard candies, sugarless gums, carrot sticks, fruit juices, and other healthy goodies to keep his mouth busy. Distract him by going for long walks or watching a movie together. Steer him clear of activities that may tempt him to smoke (e.g., drinking alcohol or going to parties). If he used smoking as a way to relieve stress, help him find other stress-busting strategies such as exercise, meditation, or massage.

• **Don't let your man give up on giving up.** Most smokers have to make several attempts to quit before they totally go off cigarettes. If your man has a relapse, be patient, supportive, and loving. Take a deep breath and help him go through the previous steps again.

For more information on helping your man to quit smoking, I strongly urge you to check out the American Cancer Society's excellent website at www.cancer.org/tobacco/quitting.html.

How to keep your man healthy and well (and beautiful!)

Hopefully, everything you read in this book will contribute toward keeping your man healthy and well—even the seemingly nonhealth-related stuff like picking out ties for him. Because when it comes right down to it, looking good, feeling good, and being healthy are completely intertwined.

It all starts with your man taking that first crucial step, whether it's making a commitment to eating well, making the decision to stop smoking, or making a trip to the Macy's menswear sale. If your man incorporates *just one positive change* into his life, it is sure to trigger more positive changes. He'll feel healthier and happier. *You'll* feel healthier and happier. The circle will keep going around. The cornucopia will keep yielding fruit.

With that in mind—and ties and menswear sales aside for the moment—here are nine very important rules for your man to follow:

- **No smoking!**

- **Don't abuse alcohol or drugs.**

- **Eat well.**

- **Exercise.**

- **Reduce stress.**

• **Get eight hours of sleep each night.**

• **Wear sunscreen.**

• **Go to the doctor for check-ups and as needed.**

• **Stop doing stupid macho stuff like not wearing bike helmets, not wearing seat belts, and driving way too fast.**

Oh, and one last rule: Be nice to your woman. Because she's the one who loves you so darned much that she's going to help you follow the other nine rules for the rest of your life.

Chapter Five

Carl wore the slippers for two weeks until one day
they had an unfortunate "accident"
involving the garbage disposal.

Dressing Your Man

Catherine, 66, thinks that her husband, Ed, 70, could use some help in the wardrobe department:

> *He has no color sense, and he hates to shop. Sometimes he comes home and I say, "Don't tell me that's what you wore today!"*

Twenty-seven-year-old Miranda is a clothes hound. And although she's generally pleased with her husband, Garrett's, attire, they can have their differences of opinion. Her fashion input can be a sore point between them:

> *We had a huge fight once because he insisted on wearing sweat pants to the mall. I was going to Nordstrom's to return a Kate Spade purse. He still wouldn't change, even though I told him we were going to a really nice department store. I said I wasn't going with him dressed like that. Needless to say, we didn't go to the mall that day.*

Women have a range of issues when it comes to their men's choice of clothes. Some of them want their men to look more hip and fashionable. ("I would love it if I could get him to wear Kenneth Cole, but he won't.") Some of them want their men to pick out colors and styles that are more flattering. ("I wish he realized that he looks terrible in black!") Some of them want their men to primp for them once in a while. ("I wish he were more willing to get dressed up for a night out at a special restaurant.") Some of them would settle for . . . well, clean clothes. ("He has a favorite pair of ripped, stained jeans. I'm mortified when he shows up in them!")

There are many reasons why a woman might be concerned about her man's attire.

• **She wants her man to succeed in life.** This woman knows that, rightly or wrongly, people are often judged on the basis of their appearance. She wants her man to replace his ill-fitting jackets, frayed pants, and less-than-flattering ties with the appropriate Power Look so he can command the kind of respect and attention he deserves at the office.

• **She wants her man to feel good about himself.** Looking good can often translate into feeling good. You want your man to wear clothes that will make him stand taller, put a smile on his face, and make him think to himself, "Damn, I look good!"

• **She wants to feel like she's still special to him.** When they were first dating, her man always wore a jacket and tie. Now, after years of marriage, he hangs out in the house in a Bud Lite T-shirt and stained sweat pants, and when they go out at night, it's like pulling teeth to get him to put on a nice button-down shirt. To her, this means that she's not "worth" looking good for anymore.

• **She doesn't find him sexy.** What's your first response when you see your honey in a black tuxedo? If you're like a lot of women, you want to have sex with him immediately. Conversely, what's your first response when you see your honey in a Bud Lite T-shirt and stained sweat pants? Probably the opposite. Okay, so a man doesn't have to wear a tuxedo every day (although wouldn't that be great?), but it would be nice if he could dress in a way that would make him more touchable, kissable, and, well, you know.

• **She wants fashion to be a priority for him.** When this woman talks about "catching up on her reading," she means *Vogue* and *Harper's Bazaar*. Her idea of heaven is a Dolce & Gabbana sale. This woman is a fashion plate, and she would like her man to be one, too.

Of course, some women just don't care about their men's attire. "Health and fitness are so much more important than clothes," said one woman. "Who needs to cave in to all that Madison Avenue pressure?" said another. And one woman said of her husband: "He's not the world's greatest dresser, but neither am I. He can wear jeans and a T-shirt for work every day, and that's fine with me."

But if the way your man dresses is *not* fine with you—and if you find that the phrases "Sweetie, that tie *really, really* doesn't match the rest of your outfit" or "Isn't it time we threw out that shirt with the holes?" can trigger World War III—read on.

Men's style 101

In order to assist your man in the attire department, it's important to start with some basics about men's style. By "style," we're not talking about helping your man dress as if he were a

GQ model (although if that's what you both want, go for it!). We're talking about helping your man dress in a way that expresses who he is, flatters his appearance, and still makes him feel like "one of the guys."

Sound simple? It is. So why are there so many men running around looking, well, less than put together?

"In the last 20 years, American men have probably spent more money on clothes than in all of history," says men's style expert Alan Flusser. "If dressing well were an issue of being able to afford good clothes, we'd have a lot of good-looking men around."

But we don't. Says Flusser, "This is a tremendous paradox."

Flusser is the author of several books on men's style, including *Style and the Man* and his latest, *Dressing the Man: Permanent Fashion*. He is also a men's custom clothing designer. In the movie *Wall Street*, the cool suits and gorgeous shirts were Flusser's work.

Not so long ago, Flusser says, it wasn't considered *manly* for men to be too interested in what they wore. Things have changed in that respect, and now, more and more men are embracing clothing as a way of communicating status, personality, and mood to the outside world.

Unfortunately, as in other modes of communication, men can be from Mars when it comes to their wardrobes. "Men *like* clothes," says Flusser. "They're just confused. Dressing well is like building a house. If you don't have a sound foundation, when the first storm comes along, the walls will fall down."

So what *is* that foundation? Flusser is unequivocal on this point. "It has nothing to do with how much money you spend. It has nothing to do with quality. It has to do with *proportion* and *color*. If you don't know about proportion and color, you can buy all the clothes in the world, and you won't look good."

Proportion: One size does not fit all

Okay, so what the heck is proportion? It is the relationship between a garment and your man's body. Simply put, good proportion means good fit.

If a piece of clothing doesn't fit, it's just not going to look right, no matter how well-designed and fabulous it is. "If you buy the finest-quality navy blazer but the proportion isn't correct, you can throw away all $4,000 of it," says Flusser. ($4,000? Gulp!)

Here are some basic rules of proportion for you and your man to keep in mind:

Suit jackets and sport coats:

• To determine if the jacket is long enough, try one of Flusser's favorite methods. Have your man put his arms down straight. The bottom of the jacket should line up with his thumb knuckle. Also—and this is crucial!—the back of the jacket should cover the curve of your man's cute little (or not-so-little) behind.

• The sleeve should just hit your man's wrist bone. Half an inch of his shirt cuff should stick out.

• Likewise, make sure that half an inch of your man's shirt collar is visible above the jacket collar.

• More on the "half-an-inch" theme: The waist button should fall half an inch below your man's natural waist. To figure out where that is, put your hands around the smallest part of his torso. Feel free to turn this into a fun tickling game!

Pants:

• The bottom of your man's pants should rest on the tops of his shoes, with a slight break in the fabric just above the cuff. (The "break" business means that if you look at his pants from the side, they will go straight down, then kind of cave in softly in the ankle area due to the action of the pants hitting the shoes.)

• According to Flusser, cuffs should be 1-5/8" if your man is under 5'10". If he is taller, go with 1-3/4".

• Pleats should lie flat. If they gape open, the pants are too tight for your man.

• The creases should go down the middle of each kneecap and finish at the middle of each shoe.

Dress shirts:

• Your man should not buy a dress shirt that fits him exactly. It will shrink!

• Close the top button of a new (i.e., unwashed) dress shirt. You should be able to slide two fingers between your man's neck and the collar.

• The sleeves must be long enough so your man can bend his arms without pulling on the cuffs. But the cuffs have to be snug enough that they don't fall over his hands.

• The shirt itself should be long enough that your man can raise his arms in the air without pulling it out of his pants. (More tickling games!)

• Traditional American shirts tend to be cut very full in the torso. European shirts tend to be more tapered. There are also some brands that offer "full" and "tapered" options. Keep this in mind, depending on whether your man is a big guy or on the slim side.

Color him beautiful

Flusser's other golden rule of style is color.

There are many schools of thought and many fun little sayings about color ("Yellow is cheerful!" "Red stands for passion!"). Some men just like to wear their favorite colors, whatever they are, because that gives them a feeling of self-confidence. Some men swear by the rule of wearing clothes to match their eye color—e.g., an emerald-green shirt to go with emerald-green eyes.

Flusser's take on color is simple and begins with a basic belief: Clothes should direct the viewer's attention to the face of the person wearing the clothes. According to him, the right color clothing will direct the viewer's eye up to your man's face. The wrong colors will wash out your man's face or otherwise spoil the overall effect.

In Flusser's color world, your man is either a *contrast* person or a *tonal* person. If he's contrast, that means his hair color and skin color are in contrast to each other (e.g., black hair and light-colored skin). If he's tonal, that means his hair color and skin color are similar (e.g., blond hair and light-colored skin).

"If you put a tonal person in high-contrast colors, it will distract from the face," Flusser says. For example, if your man is blond and fair-skinned and you put a black shirt on him—black being in high contrast to his face—then "his face is going to disappear," says Flusser.

On the other hand, "If you put a contrast person in tonal colors, it will not make his face look invigorating or fresh or youthful. It will dilute his presentation," says Flusser. So if your guy is a contrast guy, go for bright rather than muted colors.

Some final style tips

So remember the two golden rules: proportion and color. If you can pin down what proportions and colors look good on your man, you're more than halfway there!

Here are some final tips from Flusser on what you can do for your man's wardrobe:

• **Clip out magazine pictures of men's outfits and share them with your man.** "People learn to dress well by looking at other people dressing well," says Flusser. One way to achieve this is by getting a stack of men's magazines—*GQ, Men's Health, Esquire*—and cutting out photos of those hunky male models modelling clothes. Tell your honey that you're planning ahead for his birthday or the holidays and you want to get a sense of what he'd like.

• **Watch Fred Astaire movies.** You're probably thinking, "But I want my man to dress well, not learn to tap dance!" Flusser maintains that the 1930s were the height of male style and elegance. Everyone, from politicians and Hollywood stars to the average working Joe, knew how to wear clothes. Part of the reason is that most guys followed the male paradigm of tie/shirt/jacket—which for many style experts was, is, and will forever be the most flattering male paradigm of all. The other reason is that unlike today, there were so many positive role models for men's style. Watching Fred Astaire movies (or other movies from the 1930s and 1940s) will give you and your man an idea of how they did it. So pop some popcorn, put *Swingtime* into your VCR, and pay close attention!

• **Master the paradigm.** More on that tie/shirt/jacket business. Have you ever noticed a guy—maybe not your own—walking down the street in a great-fitting dark suit, crisp white shirt, dark tie, dark socks and shoes, and white handkerchief? He doesn't have to be good-looking. But he looks *soooo* good. As a homework assignment, Flusser suggests that you and your man go to a nice men's clothing store and have him try on that combo, paying careful attention to proportion (remember all the "half an inch" stuff from above). If you and he can master this paradigm, you and he can master just about anything (when it comes to clothes, that is).

• **But remember, it doesn't have to take a lot of money to dress your man well!** "There are more well-designed clothes today than there were 30 years ago," says Flusser. You can go to The Gap, Banana Republic, or any number of not-too-expensive places and buy really good stuff. Flusser says that online and catalog shopping are fine, too—as long as you're paying careful attention to proportion and color.

• **Focus on style, not fashion.** Clothes are *fashionable* in relation to a certain time period—e.g., this year. Clothes are *stylish* in relation to an individual—e.g., your man. "Fashion isn't as interesting as style," Flusser says. Help your man develop his own style, and you will have given him a precious and permanent gift.

Beware of these style landmines!

Glenn O'Brien, the "Style Guy" columnist for *GQ* and author of *The Style Guy: The Answers to the Questions Men Are Asking on Sex, Manners, Grooming, Fashion, Travel, Women, and the Meaning of Life*, offers his take on some common menswear blunders:

- *American Gigolo* **was then—this is now.** "A lot of men are stuck in the 1980s. They tend to wear these 1980s-style power suits with big shoulders and blousy pants. Women should encourage their men to wear suits with flat-front pants and a more natural shoulder look."

- **Don't cheap out on suits.** "When you're paying more for a suit, there's a reason for it. If you buy a suit that's $600, it's glued together. When that suit goes to the dry cleaner's, pretty soon, the glue's going to come apart. It's going to have bubbles in it. And it's going to look really bad. When you buy a $1,500 suit, it's probably going to be hand-made and hand-basted. It's going to look good for a long time."

- **Don't cheap out on shoes.** "You can tell the most about a man from his shoes. Pretentious men will spend a lot of money on their suits and ties and shirts, but for some reason, they're reluctant to buy good shoes."

- **Hey, where's the flood?** "A lot of men wear their pants too short, even successful businessmen. Generally, a man's trousers should break on his shoes. The only exception would be slim, high-fashion pants, which wouldn't break at all."

- **Don't ignore your body type.** "Bigger guys and heavier guys look better in single-breasted suits. You have to have a fairly good figure to carry off a double-breasted suit. Also, bigger, heavier guys look better in a two-button suit than in a three-button suit. If you're skinny, don't wear things that are too tight. And unless you're *really* skinny, stay away from shoulder pads. I prefer a more natural look."

• **Don't ignore your age.** "We have this phony youth culture where everyone wants to look younger. The English have a saying about this: 'Mutton dressed as lamb.' As kids, we wanted to grow up and look like men. Now, men want to look like kids. There's nothing to be gained there."

• **Are your shoes too casual for your outfit?** "A lot of guys will wear shoes that are too casual for their clothes—like penny loafers with a gray double-breasted suit, white shirt, and tie. That's not appropriate."

• **Keep the hockey jerseys to a minimum.** "I personally have a thing against wearing athletic uniforms as casual wear. Warm-ups on an airplane—that's really uncivilized."

• **Enough with the low-riders.** "A mistake a lot of American men make is that their pants don't come up high enough on their bodies. This is partly the fault of the clothing makers. English men make fun of American men for this—America is the country of 'the plumber's butt.' Men's pants should come up to around their navels."

• **Stop underdressing in bad weather.** "It looks so stupid— guys without raincoats when it's raining, guys without hats or overcoats when it's 30 degrees out. Maybe it's a macho thing."

• **And here's a final word of advice to women about their men:** "Don't let them wear adjustable baseball caps!"

Why your man hates to go clothes-shopping

When it comes to developing a sense of style and dressing well, shopping can often be a man's downfall. Why?

First, let's take a look at shopping from *our* perspective.

I think it's safe to generalize that women like clothes-shopping more than men. I know women who relax, rejuvenate, and de-stress by going shopping, as if trying on one not-quite-right outfit after another in a sweaty-smelling fitting room was the equivalent of getting a facial. I know women whose idea of a good contact sport is fighting other women for the best stuff at semi-annual sales. I know women who take as much pride in "never paying full price" as they would in winning the Nobel Prize.

In general, women are raised to be more appearance-conscious than men. As girls, we are taught this by our parents, our peers, and society in general. We can't pick up a magazine, turn on the TV, or watch a movie without getting hit with the message that we are supposed to be attractive, put together, and stylish—and furthermore, that picking out clothes and making up our faces can actually be fun and fulfilling—*and* help us bond with others of our gender.

Guys, on the other hand, are taught to be more focused on their achievements (i.e., achievements other than scoring Armani at wholesale). And when it comes to clothes-shopping as adults, a guy can often flash back in terror to his days of clothes-shopping with Mom: navigating the aisles of Sears and Montgomery Ward and Penney's; having to stand in his Fruit-of-the-Looms in front of some strange salesman; Mom making him try on dozens of geeky-looking cotton-poly shirts and cardboard-stiff cords.

And practically speaking, it's *not* easy for guys to shop these days. In a December 1, 2000, *Wall Street Journal* article by Sam

Walker, the headline and tagline read: *"Fashion's Latest Victims: Men.* Men's clothing sales are growing faster than women's for the first time. So why aren't retailers giving guys more respect? From shrinking store space to cuff links that don't fit into shirts, the industry is alienating some of the customers it needs most."

Men are spending more money than ever on clothes that don't fit, don't look good, and don't match. They're finding that even the finest department stores don't have enough sales staff—or enough *competent* sales staff—to assist them. No wonder many of them dread a trip to the menswear department as much as a trip to the dentist's office.

Fortunately, that's where you—the woman—can come to the rescue.

Shopping with your man

"Women are more used to making choices in their wardrobe than men are," says Glenn O'Brien. "Women can help them exercise choice. Women can help them coordinate color."

"I always go clothes-shopping with him, and he appreciates my help," says 28-year-old Sandy of her 30-year-old husband, Rob. "Matching stuff freaks him out, and he trusts my opinions."

Like Sandy and Rob, maybe you and your man are already in the habit of shopping together. If the process is always smooth sailing—i.e., you and your man are happy with the clothes you end up buying for him—congratulations! But if not, here are some tips to consider:

• **Find good help.** The next time you and your man go shopping, encourage him to ask for direction (not *directions*—that's a subject for another book!). According to many style experts, the best way to shop successfully is to find a salesperson you can trust at a store you can trust—and then maintain a lasting relationship with him. Alan Flusser offers this advice to men: "Look for a salesperson who is dressed the way you would like to be dressed—or close to it. Then ask him, 'I'm looking for some clothes. What would you recommend?' " This strategy is especially important for pricier garments. Says Flusser, "If I'm going to buy a suit from a salesperson, he'd better have on a suit and tie and shirt that look pretty great."

• **Let him see for himself.** "My boyfriend used to be obsessed with wearing really trendy-looking clothes," says 34-year-old Olivia. "But a lot of it didn't look good on him. One day, while we were at Bloomingdale's, I picked out some more classic-looking pieces for him and asked him to try them on—you know, 'just for the heck of it.' When he did, he could see for himself that they were way more flattering on him." If your man is used to dressing a certain way—maybe a certain *un-attractive* way—it may take more than your word to make him shift gears. Steer him gently in a new direction, then let the dressing-room mirror do the rest of the talking.

• **Be selective.** You know that awful feeling you get when you look in your closet and realize that it's full of stuff you've never worn—and never will? Or that *other* awful feeling you get when you look in your closet and realize that it's full of stuff that fell apart after three washings? Keep that in mind when you go shopping with your man. Convince him that it's *so* much better to buy quality items that will last than to spend the same amount of money on less-than-quality items that will never get worn. Convince him, too, that the higher-priced clothes will pay for themselves over time. O'Brien has suits he's been wearing for 12 years, shirts he's been wearing for 20 years, and ties he's been wearing for 30 years. His advice? "Buy intelligently."

• **Keep your eyes open for sales.** Maybe it's my X chromosome talking, but sales can be a great way to get a lot more for a lot less. Good times to look for major markdowns are in late January, after the holiday rush is over, and in early August, before serious fall shopping commences. Just remember that during big sales, you and your man will probably encounter overcrowded aisles, overextended staff, and long lines for the dressing rooms. Also remember that sales tend to fuel impulse-buying ("Ohmigod, honey, those black leather pants are 60 percent off!"). Stick to the stuff your man really wants and needs.

• **Make sure that your man comes prepared.** If your man is buying a suit, sportcoat, or pants, he should bring the items he usually carries on his person—wallet, sunglasses case, Mont Blanc pens, big jangly keychain—and stuff them into the appropriate pockets and compartments of whatever he's trying on. A bulge here or a bulge there might throw off the fit of a garment, which needs to be taken into account.

• **Remember that he's a guy.** Huh? You're thinking, isn't that what this whole book is about? The point is, personal variations aside, men tend to want to look pretty much the same as other men. Consider this example: If a woman walks into a party wearing a new dress and sees that several other women are wearing the same dress, she will probably be mortified because she doesn't stand out. On the other hand, if a man walks into a party wearing a gray suit, white shirt, and blue tie and sees that several other men are wearing the exact same combo, he will probably be pleased because he fits in.

How to Get a Custom-Made Suit for a Ready-Made Price

O'Brien offers this little-known tip for those with access to big-city department stores—and big budgets. Twice a year, Saks Fifth Avenue, Barney's, Bergdorf's, and other carriers of menswear will hold a "trunk show," where your man can get a suit to measure for the same price as an off-the-rack suit. Custom-made suits are especially suited (excuse the pun!) to men who don't have "off-the-rack" bodies and require a lot of finicky tailoring. Keep your eyes open for advertisements, or call the stores. And remember, it's still not going to be cheap—we're probably talking a thousand dollars and up per suit.

Keep this in mind when you're shopping together and you're tempted to hand him neon-orange shirts and orchid-print ties to try on. Your honey wants to look attractive—not attract attention.

• **Don't act like his mommy.** This one doesn't require too much explanation, right? *Right????* It's crucially important that your man doesn't feel like he's 11 years old and back at Sears with his mother. ("You *have* to get these slacks for your piano recital!") Make shopping together a fun, funny, sexy experience. Have piña coladas before you set out. At the store, make jokes about other customers, about bad salespeople, about your mothers. If you can, sneak into the dressing room with him and give him some hands-on help. If you can't, whisper in his ear how much you wish you *could*.

Don't Take Him Shoe-Shopping Before Lunch

The best time to buy shoes is in the afternoon, because feet tend to swell during the course of the day. At the shoe store, make sure your man gets his feet measured properly, and make sure he gets both the right and left feet measured, as they can be slightly different.

Shopping without your man

Some men prefer that their women do all their shopping. ("My wife buys *all* my clothes, and that's just fine with me," says Russ, 38.) Some men are willing to do their own shopping, but their women wish it were otherwise. ("I close my eyes and hold my breath every time he comes home from the mall," says 30-something Leslie about her 40-something boyfriend, Kyle.)

Whether you're doing damage control on your man's wardrobe or relieving him of a task he doesn't particularly enjoy, here are some tips to help you shop successfully for your man—on your own:

• **Stick to your man's established brands, sizes, and styles.** Remember all that stuff I discussed about the importance of proportion and fit? It's not enough to go to the store with your man's sizes, since designations like "Extra-Large" and "42L" aren't going to be the same from maker to maker. If possible, convince your man to go on a couple of shopping expeditions with you to determine what brands, sizes, and styles look good on him. Then continue replenishing those items on your own. (Needless to say, you can probably finesse socks, underwear, and other similar items with just a list of his sizes.)

• **If you can't bring the man to the mall, bring the mall to the man.** "He *hates* to shop. Loathes it," says 27-year-old Miranda about her 30-year-old husband, Garrett. "He'd rather go to someone's funeral, I think. So I'll go to Banana Republic and bring home $300 worth of clothes. He'll pick out a shirt or two and a pair of jeans, then one of us takes the rest back. It works out well. I get to pick out the coolest clothes, but he still chooses the ones he likes. We're both happy." Like Miranda, if you have your husband's basic sizes and tastes down, then you can do 90 percent of the shopping for him—and take advantage of those generous return policies.

• **Make a game out of it.** Remember Cheryl, whose ex-husband, Dan, stapled his clothes on their second date? She somehow managed to get past that little incident, and their relationship progressed. She planned to introduce him to her family in Connecticut—but not in stapled clothes! "I went on a shopping spree for him," she said. "Then I put the clothes in boxes and hid the boxes around his house. I left clues on his mirror, his refrigerator—Post-it notes saying things like 'NEED A SHIRT?' He found the boxes, and he loved it! He was a little embarrassed at first, but he said it made him feel loved. He told me, 'I never had anyone care enough about me to care about how I look.' "

• **Sneak it in.** If you gradually and quietly replace the things in your man's closet, he might not notice—or he might, and feel happily motivated to do more. Witness this story, which a friend of mine told me about a 60-something woman named Jill: "Jill was introduced to Jerome on a blind date. He wore gold chains, open-collar polyester shirts, and had a skinny little mustache over his lip . . . not her style, to say the least. But he was a great guy under all that, and she grew to care for him.

So as they dated and she started spending the nights at his place, every time she went there she would replace a polyester shirt in his closet with a 100 percent cotton button-down shirt. She bought him ties whenever she could. Soon the mustache went, and the chains along with it, and he became quite the dapper-looking guy. Within 18 months they got married. That was 15 years ago, and they're still as happy as could be."

• **Model it for him.** If your man is not big on gifts of clothing, try this trick. Buy him a great new shirt. When the two of you are getting ready to go to bed, come out of the bathroom wearing it—and nothing else. Say, "Honey, I bought you a little something today. Do you like it?" See if he complains.

Shopping with a personal shopper

If you're lucky enough to be in a city with a major department store, you may have the answer to all your men's clothes-shopping prayers: the personal shopper.

Some department stores will have a personal shopper (or two or three) on staff. A personal shopper can help your man build or enhance his wardrobe—at no extra charge.

"Our job is to make a man's shopping experience time-efficient and cost-efficient," says Marvin Piland.

Piland is the manager of the Fifth Avenue Club for Men at Saks Fifth Avenue in New York City. He and two other staff members provide personal shopping services for Saks Fifth Avenue customers.

The beauty of personal shopping is that a man can come in at an appointed time and have a knowledgeable salesperson wait exclusively on him. With this kind of one-on-one attention—plus private fitting areas—the personal shopping experience is the *opposite* of, say, fighting for help and changing-room turf during a massive semi-annual sale.

And in case you were wondering: Personal shopping isn't just for the rich and famous. According to Piland, their clients represent a range of professions and income levels—not just CEOs but "men who might be CEOs in 10 years."

Before the first visit, a personal shopper will probably have a phone interview with a potential client. "We'll ask a bunch of questions," says John O'Malley, who works for Piland. "Like: What kind of business are you in? Do you live in the city or the country? What have you worn in the past? Do you consider yourself a conservative dresser? What are you looking for?"

Once a personal shopper has a good understanding of a client's lifestyle, tastes, sizes, color preferences, and so forth, he can preselect a range of clothing and have them laid out for the first appointment. "We try to anticipate what he needs," says Piland. "If we can organize things ahead of his visit and have everything color-coordinated, we can generally assemble a spring or fall wardrobe in an hour and a half."

While the client is there, Piland and O'Malley try to educate him about clothing—why some styles might become him, why other styles might not. But mostly they try to let the "mirror do the talking."

"A lot of the guys come in here like, 'I want an Armani suit,'" O'Malley says.

"But Armani may not be the correct thing for him," Piland explains. "We don't tell him that, though. We let him put it on, and he can see it. Then we put something else on him—like a Zegna—and he can see the difference for himself. There is a moment of truth when a man looks in the mirror, and all of a sudden, what you have told him and you have shown him and what he

Personal Shopping—At a Price

Some personal shoppers are not affiliated with a store but work on their own—and consequently charge for their services. Be sure to ask about fees before signing on.

is seeing come together. That's when he begins to enjoy the process."

"All of a sudden, it's, 'Hey! I can do this! I look good!' " adds O'Malley. "It's a transformation."

Piland and his staff work with out-of-towners who are visiting New York as well as clients who have moved out of the area. As long as there is an initial visit to establish the relationship, they can continue providing service to the client long-distance.

And while the emphasis is on wardrobe-building, once the relationship is established, no request is considered too small.

"There is no minimum. One of our clients called the other day and asked to have six pairs of socks delivered to his office," Piland says. "And we did it."

How to dress your man in style for work

By now, your man probably knows the appropriate "uniform" for his job—whether it's a suit and tie, button-down shirt and khakis, or T-shirt and jeans. Whatever the case, you can help him dress more stylishly so that he looks good, feels good, and commands respect:

- **Get your own picture of his "uniform."** What do his male co-workers wear? If he has a male boss, what does *he* wear?

Your man is going to want to take his cues from them because he will want to fit in—not stand out. But while he may only have a vague idea of what's appropriate ("some sort of jacket and tie thing Monday through Thursday, and jeans and whatever on casual Fridays"), you may be able to pick up other pieces of information that will be useful for him—e.g., the bigwigs favor navy and gray; the fast-track guys wear a jacket even on casual Fridays.

• **Help him navigate the morning rush hour.** Mornings can be a crazy time, with kids to get ready for school, breakfast to be made, and all that general morning chaos. Ease your man's morning routine by laying out clothes for him the night before. Make sure that everything has been properly cleaned and pressed (whether by him, you, or the neighborhood cleaner). If he prefers to pick out his own outfit and the outfit needs tweaking, tweak in a gentle, positive way. ("You look so sexy in that green tie I gave you. Why don't you wear it instead of the red one?" "Oh my gosh, those shoes need shining, and I meant to deal with that yesterday. I'm so sorry! Why don't you wear your other pair of black shoes instead?")

• **Take advantage of the morning after.** Just because you and your man don't live together doesn't mean you can't help him look "put together" on weekday mornings. Says 25-year-old Lisa of her 33-year-old boyfriend, Eric: "When we are together in the morning, I always help him pick out what to wear. He is very receptive to my suggestions." Forty-four-year-old Susana recalls a time before she and 56-year-old husband, Frank, were married. "His co-workers knew when he had been at my house or me at his the night before by the way he was dressed. His more stylish attire was the telltale sign."

• **And just in case . . .** Encourage your man to keep a freshly
laundered extra shirt and tie at his office.

How to dress your man in casual style

Things were so much simpler back in the days when a suit and
tie were required attire for guys. With the advent of "casual"
(thanks a lot, Bill Gates!), men are in a state of confusion. What
is casual, anyway? Does that mean khakis or jeans? Button-down
shirt or T-shirt? Jacket or no jacket? Leather shoes or Reeboks?

"Now that this 'casual' thing has come in, men are completely
perplexed," says Glenn O'Brien. "They know how to wear the
uniform. That's what they grew up with: the fraternity uniform,
the pinstripe-suit uniform. But when they have to exercise choice,
they don't know what to do."

Here are some good casual options for your guy, whether it's
for casual Fridays at the office or Friday nights out with you:

• A jacket or sportcoat has many, many advantages (plus, it
can always be taken off if your man feels overdressed). It will
"finish" the outfit. It can make a big guy look slimmer, and a
slim guy look bigger. It will be kinder to your man's less-than-
buff waistline than a shirt-only look, which will draw a person's eyes right smack to that area.

• A great sweater can help pull a look together, too. A cardigan
can often be substituted for a jacket. A V-neck is attractive and
versatile, working equally well with a shirt/tie/jacket/slacks
combo as with a nice T-shirt/jeans combo. Ditto with a crew
neck. Opt for natural fabrics like cashmere, wool, silk, and cot-

ton. A small percentage of polyester or acrylic in the overall fabric content is fine, but stay away from 100 percent synthetic.

• When it comes to pants, your man is always safe with dress slacks, khakis, or chinos. A pair of well-fitting jeans can be appropriate for many casual situations. Save the shorts for around the house, the pool, the beach, picnics, super-informal parties, and running errands on a hot day.

• Some safe shirt choices: oxford button-down shirts, denim shirts, polo shirts, and banded-collar shirts. Make sure the style and fit are flattering to your man. If your man insists on wearing a T-shirt, it should be plain, solid-colored, high-quality, and *very, very clean.*

• *Under no circumstances* should your man equate "casual" with "sloppy." That means nothing stained, frayed, or falling apart at the seams.

And finally: Women often complain about their men hanging out in the house in ratty sweats, shorts, and T-shirts (or, God forbid, tank shirts). We understand that our men want to be comfortable. But comfortable doesn't have to mean ratty.

Says Juliana, 37: "My husband has nice, comfy clothes that he will wear only at home. Not dirty old sweat pants, but a couple of Adidas pants and nice, relaxed-fit sweatshirts or T-shirts. I think it makes a difference when a man cares about his appearance at home and is not sloppy."

How to dress your man in style for a night out on the town

"It is pretty common that I am dressed nicely to go out on the town and he is in jeans," complains Amy, 25, about her boyfriend of three years. "He doesn't look dirty, but he doesn't look well put together, either."

No doubt a lot of guys would make their wives and girlfriends very, very happy if they'd dress up for dates, dinner parties, and other special occasions. But some of them are completely resistant. Sally, 42, describes her 44-year-old husband, Derek's, views on dressing up this way: "His attitude: 'Sure, I'd renew our vows after 25 years, as long as I get to wear jeans.'"

It's hard to get a leopard to change his spots. And your man may feel genuinely uncomfortable in anything but "extreme casual." But here are some ways you might be able to "tweak him up" the next time you go out:

- **Learn the five most important words in the English language.** As you're getting dressed for an evening out, say, "You look so sexy in" . . . fill in the blank . . . then ask him to wear it for you.

- **Make it about you.** Tell him that you hate to impose on him, but you *really, really* want to wear that low-cut, backless black cocktail dress that he likes so much, but you don't want to feel overdressed, so could he possibly do you a favor and wear a jacket and tie?

- **Reorganize his closet.** Some men dislike picking out outfits for going out, but they don't exactly want you to do it for them (bad flashbacks to Mommy). Give him some behind-the-scenes help by reorganizing his clothes: casual stuff on the right, dressier stuff on the left. Hopefully, he will learn to associate "left side" with a broad-brush category of special occasions: parties, weddings, anniversaries, dinners out, and so forth.

• **Compromise.** Okay, so he can wear the jeans. But maybe he could pair them with a crisp white shirt, black merino wool V-neck sweater, sport jacket, socks, and black loafers. In the summer, it could be a linen shirt with a lightweight jacket.

• **It doesn't have to be a $2,000-dollar suit.** "When we didn't have to spend a lot of money on clothes, Karl bought a shark skin sports jacket for $12 at a consignment store," says Juliana, 37. "He wore it to many parties, and it saved us from buying expensive, boring jackets. You don't need a lot of money to dress well—just imagination and style."

Glasses, accessories, and other extras

Here are some tips on a few very important items that will "finish" your man's look:

• **Glasses.** If your man has a round face, go for squared-off frames. If he has a square face, go for round frames. If your man has a pointy chin, go for frames with heavy temple pieces. If your man has an oval face, he'll look good in just about anything.

• **Belts.** Your man's belt should match his shoes. It should also be darker than the clothes he's wearing. Top-of-the-line belts will be made of full-grain leather, lizard, snakeskin, alligator, or crocodile. Split cowhide is lower-end stuff. Buckles should be made of brass or silver; they should *not* be big and bulging, unless your man wants to draw attention to his torso region.

• **Hats.** Hats are often a matter of personal taste. Of course, they also serve to keep your man's head warm in inclement weather. For practical wintertime needs, look for caps made of wool or polarfleece, with or without earflaps. For fun, your man might want to try an Irish walking cap, a cowboy hat, a beret, or a straw Panama. For true old-fashioned elegance, buy your man a fedora or a homburg.

• **Outerwear.** At minimum, your man needs a down-filled parka, a raincoat (preferably a good trench coat with a removable lining), and a wool or cashmere overcoat. A leather jacket would be icing on the cake. For overcoats, midcalf-length is traditional and classic and is good for the office or for going out. Knee-length is more casual. Your man should go with an overcoat that's one size larger than his suit size. Make sure he has leather gloves, warm ski gloves, and plenty of silk and wool scarves to go with his outerwear.

Confessions of a stylish slacker

Liam, 29, is a self-described "middle-class white guy." He says he'd love to get dressed up once in a while—but feels that he can't, given the way other guys dress. Here's what he says:

> *Every guy looks the same.*
> *They all dress the same. All guys' clothing stores are the same. All guys have the same wardrobes.*
> *Sure, every guy wants to walk into the room and think that*

the ladies think HE'S the good-looking one. You don't want to look like a lame Joe. But guys want to look the same as each other, and they have difficulty distinguishing themselves within that sameness.

The thing is, it's easier for guys to look good these days. Nice clothes are more affordable. There are more products available. But GUYS LOOK MUCH WORSE THAN THEY USED TO. They dress completely inappropriately for events. They dress like they're on their way to the gym.

Guys want to fit in. On the one hand you want to look good; you want to be impressive; you want to feel good. On the other hand, you want to be a guy's guy—you don't want to walk into a room overdressed. You want to relate on a common level to other guys. They won't accept you as a guy if their first impression is that you're some mamby-pamby in loafers. That's not a guy's guy—it's an immediate stigma.

If I wear slacks to play golf, the guys will be like, "What are you all dressed up for?" I tell them, "I don't want to dress like a bum."

I wish there were more occasions to dress up. But if we're going out to dinner with friends, 99 percent of the guys won't be dressed up. Especially in the summer, my friends are going to have shorts and sandals on. Or flip-flops—give me a break.

There's a uniform for slacker guys—khakis and a polo shirt. Or one of those free beer logo shirts. I don't like the polo shirts—too wide in the collar. Looks dorky if they're buttoned to the top, and when they're open, you look too "white guy." But I wear those things because that's the uniform.

It's tough to know what kind of shirt to wear if you're a guy. One little thing, and you're too dressed up. A lot of times,

Americans in Paris

In his book *Me Talk Pretty One Day*, writer David Sedaris describes a couple of American tourists who have a decidedly American view of travel attire:

Because they had used the tiresome word froggy and complained about my odor, I was now licensed to hate this couple as much as I wanted. This made me happy, as I'd wanted to hate them from the moment I'd entered the subway car and seen them hugging the pole. Unleashed by their insults, I was now free to criticize Martin's clothing: the pleated denim shorts, the baseball cap, the T-shirt advertising a San Diego pizza restaurant. Sunglasses hung from his neck on a fluorescent cable, and the couple's bright new his-and-her sneakers suggested that they might be headed somewhere dressy for dinner. Comfort has its place, but it seems rude to visit another country dressed as if you've come to mow its lawns. (from Me Talk Pretty One Day *by David Sedaris, pg. 222, Little Brown & Co., 2000)*

if you wear a long-sleeve oxford shirt, you're probably too dressed up.

You can't wear a jacket anymore to go out. You feel goofy putting on a jacket. You'd rather wear an overcoat. That's why guys wear overcoats, leather coats, pea coats—some coat to finish the look. But not a jacket. I'm 29 years old and I feel too young to wear a jacket to go out. I feel like a kid.

I wish I'd grown up in the 1920s and 1930s. Everyone looked fantastic. Now we're an off-the-rack nation. Men never get anything tailored anymore. Men never even go to the dry cleaners.

How to dress (and undress) your man in style for the bedroom

Juliana, 37, is fond of her husband's bedroom attire. "I don't know what I would do if Karl stopped wearing his animal print G-strings," she says.

Well, isn't it nice to know that there are guys out there who don't wear saggy white BVDs to bed?

Just as your man would probably prefer to see you in a lacy black Victoria's Secret number or a cute little white cotton nightie, you would probably prefer to see him in something other than underwear or pajamas circa 1973.

With that in mind, here are some ideas for sexy bedtime styles for him:

• **Boxers.** With or without a nice T-shirt (no ketchup stains or rock band logos). My personal favorite boxer brands: Brooks Brothers, Calvin Klein, and The Gap.

• **Pajama bottoms only.** Seersucker or flannel, especially with a drawstring that you can untie in two seconds.

• **A nice robe.** If all he has is an old terry-cloth one that looks as though a family of cats have used it for a scratching post, it's time to throw it out and get him a new one.

• **Exotic underwear.** They're not just for us, ladies! Think animal prints, thongs, fishnet, or sheer material.

• **Anything silk.** Silk boxers, silk pajamas, and silk robes make your man oh-so-touchable.

Clothes maintenance 101

"Kevin always wore wrinkly shirts," complained Maryann, 33, of her husband. "He'd say, 'If I wear it, the wrinkles will just kinda come out on their own.' And of course they didn't!"

So Maryann took matters into her own hands. She started taking his shirts to the cleaner's every week to be professionally laundered and boxed. "The $7.50 per week was money well spent," she said. Her husband grew to like the wrinkle-free shirts in their boxes, and "Now he takes them to the cleaner's on his own."

In addition to letting the pros handle your man's shirts—truly a small price to pay for a wonderful, wonderful service—here are some tips for keeping his clothes in prime shape:

• Scan his closet once a week for items that need to be dry-cleaned, rips and seams that need to be repaired, and buttons that need to be replaced. Do (or delegate) those jobs immediately.

• Ties should never be dry-cleaned. Many dry cleaners don't have the proper equipment to deal with ties and may ruin them. The best option is to call a professional tie-cleaning service such as Tiecrafters, Inc. (252 West 29th Street, New York, NY 10001, 212-629-5800). You can send your man's tie to them (as soon as possible after he spills wine or French onion dip on it—not months and months later), and they will clean it, press and roll it, and return it to you.

• Dress shirts should never be dry-cleaned, either. Instead, buy them to allow for shrinkage, then have them laundered and pressed.

• Dry-clean your man's suits sparingly. If the suit is stained, have it professionally spot-cleaned instead, then pressed.

• Find your man a good tailor. A good tailor will be able to tweak his clothes this way and that way so they fit and flatter his body. "My tailor does more for me than my trainer," says Glenn O'Brien.

• Buy your man a lint roller for home, his car, and his office.

• More essentials for his office: a small sewing kit, some safety pins, and a bottle of spot remover.

• Keep your man's shoes polished at all times! Unpolished shoes will bring down a good outfit faster than just about anything.

• For storage purposes, your man's shoes need wooden shoe trees—not plastic ones.

• Your man's clothes need wooden hangers, not wire ones. Wishbone-style kinds are best for his jackets.

• If it's stained or frayed or torn beyond repair, throw it out—and don't look back.

Chapter Six

Larry Vulmer: the Comb-Over King.

Grooming Your Man

When it comes to grooming, women have a variety of issues about their men:

He needs to brush his teeth more often. For some reason, he feels like he doesn't need to brush his teeth until after he eats breakfast. I can't stand that! (Amy, 25, about boyfriend, Jack, 26)

I wish his nails looked better. He bites his nails. And I wish I didn't have to remind him to comb his hair. (Katie, 40, about husband, Reg, 53)

He does not wash his hands enough—after reading the newspaper or after using the bathroom! (Catherine, 66, about husband, Ed, 70)

They don't shave every day like they used to when you were dating, and when they do shave, it's to go to work. But they forget that they sleep with us and that we want a shaved face! (Gina, 33, about men in general)

Are Men the New Women?

The cover of the April 2, 2001, *New York* magazine depicted a picture of a hunky young (naked) guy staring at himself in the mirror with the tagline: "ARE MEN THE NEW WOMEN? MALE VANITY."

The story went on to suggest that today's men are just as obsessed with beauty as women and that corporate he-men are flocking to pricey spas and salons for facials, manicures, pedicures, and other specialty treatments so they can get a "competitive edge."

Good grooming habits start early in life. My own parents were less-than-careful about teaching me the basics, so I had to make up for it in my teens and 20s by imitating my friends, watching TV, and reading Cosmo. (See, that stuff *can* be educational.)

As the mother of a six-year-old boy, I'm constantly reminding him to brush his teeth, wash his hands, and comb his hair. Christopher can't quite comprehend why long, icky fingernails and toenails need to be dealt with, and our Sunday night manicures and pedicures are an ordeal for both of us. Although lately, he's started showing interest in my fancy manicure equipment—and once in a while, I will walk in on him carefully picking out dirt from under his nails with my little silver scraper.

Hopefully Christopher is learning, and hopefully his significant other will someday thank me for all this.

If you're lucky enough to be with a man who was raised by a caring mom or dad, or who developed stellar grooming skills all on his own, congratulations! (One woman wrote: "My husband has really good grooming habits. Once, he wouldn't drive me to the emergency room until he took his shower and dressed!") But if your man is less than meticulous about his teeth, hair, nails, or other body parts, read on.

Taking care of his skin

I know a lot of men who think that "skin care" means taking a shower and splashing cold water on their face—and that's it. These are *not* men who have flawless, maintenance-free skin (which doesn't exist, anyway). These men have dry skin, blemishes, and other noticeable problems that are crying out for help.

So why aren't they taking better care of their skin?

Men have the same hang-ups about skin care that they have about grooming in general. Some men are never taught about proper skin care. Some men think of skin care as a "woman's thing." Moisturizers? Cleansers? Aren't those, like, girlie products?

Uh-uh. Your honey's skin needs as much care as yours—and he needs those products, too. Tell him you want to pamper the largest organ on his body (well, maybe the *second* largest), and start doing the following:

- **The Number One Rule: Apply that sunscreen!** I can't emphasize this one enough. Exposure to UV radiation from the sun can result in prematurely aging skin, blemishes, and the dreaded C word: *Cancer*. Make sure your man applies waterproof sunscreen with a sun protection factor (SPF) of 15 or more whenever he goes out into the sun—even if it's overcast out. He should apply it half an hour before he goes out and reapply it every few hours. Make sure he has a bottle of it at home, in his car, in his gym bag, and at his office. Other sun protection strategies include staying in the shade, especially between 10 A.M. and 3 P.M.; covering up with a wide-brimmed hat (think Indiana Jones!); and donning sunglasses (but not the cheap ones you can buy on the street—stick to reputable manufacturers). Some people are sensitive to PABA. If your man is one of them, look for a PABA-free sunscreen.

- **Turn your man on to cleansing and moisturizing.** Your man should wash his face and moisturize once or twice a day with the appropriate products for his skin type (oily, normal, dry, or some combination thereof). And in case you and your man haven't noticed: There are companies out there making cleansers and moisturizers *just for men*. They don't come in pretty bottles with flowers on them—they come in manly, industrial-looking bottles that evoke WD40, metallic-looking bottles that evoke "high-tech," and super-white, super-clinical-looking bottles that evoke "science." Go to the department store or go online and shop for some of these goodies for your man. Some favorite brands of men I know: Kiehl's, Zirh, Surface, American Crew, The Body Shop, Clinique, Happy for Men, Lab Series for Men, and Aveda. If you're on a budget, a guy I know—a former model—swears by good old Nivea. Neutrogena makes great products, too. If your man's skin is sensitive, avoid products with fragrances or preservatives.

- **Turn down the temperature.** Encourage your man to avoid hot showers or baths, which can be drying. Also, after he steps out of the tub, he should apply a light moisturizer all over. (Or offer to do it for him!)

- **Don't dry out his dry skin.** Buy moisturizing soaps for the shower such as Dove or Neutrogena instead of those harsh deodorant kinds. Consider buying a humidifier or vaporizer for your house. Make sure he moisturizes regularly—especially his elbows, knees, hands, and feet, which can become super-dry. Also, if fabrics such as wool and polyester make your man's dry skin feel all itchy and irritated, dress him in cotton and silk.

- **Hydrate your man.** I first mentioned this in chapter Two, and it's worth re-mentioning here. Those eight glasses of water a day (more if it's hot out or if your man exercises a lot) are necessary to keep his skin supple, smooth, and happy. Juices and other healthy drinks are fine, too.

• **Give his skin a regular check-up.** Periodically, take off all his clothes—this is the fun part—and examine every square inch of his skin. Study his moles, freckles, and other bumps, dots, and spots. If you notice changes in the size, shape, texture, or color of any of the above—or a sore that just won't heal— make an appointment with a dermatologist ASAP.

• **Ban those blemishes.** To prevent blemishes, encourage your man to wash his face with a special cleanser made especially for blemish-prone skin.

For mild outbreaks, Dr. Mary Ellen Brademas—a New York dermatologist—recommends benzoyl peroxide combined with something called clindamycin. This topical combo is available by prescription only. There are also retinoids, such as the prescription cream Retin-A.

"More serious cases will probably require some kind of an oral antibiotic," says Dr. Brademas, whose patients are about 35 to 40 percent men.

Dr. Brademas adds that *very* serious cases might warrant the prescription medication Accutane. She explains that Accutane is fairly safe for men, although there are a number of precautions that must be observed; for example, your man has to be extremely careful about sun exposure; he has to monitor his cholesterol and triglyceride counts; he is advised not to take aspirin, aspirin-like drugs, or vitamin E; and he must watch his alcohol intake.

As far as over-the-counter remedies for blemishes go: Dr. Brademas suggests that benzoyl peroxides are effective, as are some retinol products (a retinol being a weaker form of a retinoid such as Retin-A).

Salicylic acid products are also popular for blemishes. Look for salicylic acid in lotions, creams, and pads.

• **Give your man a facial.** Don't laugh. These days, he-men are going for facials as a way of relaxing, recharging—and yes, getting rid of those nasty facial problems like blackheads, blemishes, and ingrown hairs. Some salons and spas offer facials just for men: Sports Club L.A. and SkinCareLab in New York City offer something called the "Gentleman's Facial."

You might also try giving your honey a home facial and have a Friday-night pampering session (including candles, wine, soft music, and as little clothing as possible). You can choose from a number of inexpensive facial products at the drugstore, or order some online from blissworld.com. Or mix up a batch of homemade masks: Try crushed cucumber; mashed, cooked carrot and a bit of honey; crushed orange, papaya, or pineapple; uncooked oatmeal and plain yogurt; or an egg white. Leave on his face and rinse with cool water after 10 minutes.

Botox, anyone?

"Cosmetic dermatology is becoming more popular for men," says Dr. Frederic Brandt, "especially men in their 20s, 30s, and 40s. There is more of an emphasis on men looking good these days—we see it in the magazines and on the billboards—and it's spilling over into skin care. Part of looking good is maintaining one's skin."

Dr. Brandt has a cosmetic dermatology practice in Miami and New York City. He offers a number of procedures for men, including laser resurfacing and liposuction—and less-invasive ones such as collagen injections and Botox.

Botox?

Botox is a botulism toxin that literally paralyzes certain types of wrinkles. "We do Botox injections in the forehead area, around the eyes, and in the neck," explains Dr. Brandt. "They eliminate wrinkles that are muscular in origin, like crow's feet. They lift up the brow. They lift up the face."

Dr. Brandt's patients who use Botox come in for it approximately every four months. He says that bruising can be a possible side effect, but otherwise, "there's no recuperation time. Men like things that don't have telltale signs—no scars. They want to go right back to work. They don't want their life interrupted."

Acne scars and marionette lines—those lines that extend out from the corners of the mouth—can benefit from collagen injections. As with Botox, there's no recuperation time: "In and out, wash and wear," says Dr. Brandt.

A new type of laser rejuvenation treatment offered by Dr. Brandt can help eliminate brown and red marks and scars. It's done once a month for three or four months and works by stimulating the skin cells. "You're red for a day, and that's about it," says Dr. Brandt.

Prices on these procedures will vary from practitioner to practitioner. They could set you back hundreds or thousands of dollars, depending on what procedures you need and how often they must be repeated. For more information on these procedures, you can check out the websites for the American Society for Aesthetic Plastic Surgery (www.surgery.org) or the American Society for Dermatologic Surgery (www.asds-net.org). General-health websites such as DrKoop.com can also provide good information on cosmetic dermatology procedures.

RX: Dark Circles

Eye creams containing vitamin K can lighten those permanent dark circles under your man's eyes. They work by helping heal damaged blood vessels. Rub the cream under your man's eyes before bedtime.

Taking care of his hair

Anna, 34, had a funny story about her 45-year-old husband's hair. This happened while they were still dating:

Michael had this thing about his hair. He wanted it to be long, flowing, and straight—not an easy task when you are a big Italian guy with naturally curly, curly hair that's slightly receding at the top. But Michael was determined. He would blow dry it to death and even lie on his bed during the process to get the back of it straight. Poor, confused Michael!

Anyway, I always used to wonder why Michael had this odd do. It was a very 1970s, outdated, blow-dried hairstyle that looked too primped.

One morning after we had been dating for a few months, he was running late for work. He got out of the shower and immediately asked me for the dreaded blow dryer.

"Blow dryer, gosh, I don't know, Michael," I lied.

Little did he know it was under my bed wrapped in a towel. I very innocently suggested he just let his hair dry naturally. I praised his curls with compliments. And when he came home from his job site later, he told me that even his fellow construction workers had commented, "Hey Michael, it's about time you ditched the dryer. Your hair looks much better, man." My devious plan worked, and Michael felt so much better.

RX: Undereye Bags

If your man suffers from undereye puffiness in the morning, have a tea party! Before he rushes off to work, have him lie in bed for 15 minutes with his eyes closed. Place two moist tea bags or two slices of cold cucumber over his eyes. While he's hanging out, he can listen to NPR, Rush, or Howard Stern; visualize all the good stuff he's going to accomplish that day; or have you cover his belly button with kisses—whatever passes the time!

Michael isn't alone. According to Brad Johns, "Most men don't take care of their hair properly."

Johns is Artistic Director of the Avon Salon and Spa in New York City's Trump Tower. Dubbed a "colorist extraordinaire" by *New York* magazine, his clientele include such lushly coiffed luminaries as Johnny Depp, Natasha Richardson, and supermodels Marcus Schenkenberg and James King.

"Most men don't use the right products," Johns explains. "And they don't get the right cuts. Also, a lot of men think that grooming themselves is a 'feminine thing.' So they do the minimal amount of stuff—stuff they heard through the grapevine."

Unfortunately, grapevine grooming is not always the way to go. And as a result, a man can often look less-than-put-together in a very conspicuous way. (Didn't someone once say that having bad hair is like having a room with an unmade bed?)

Johns suggests that a good stylist can offer the *right* grooming and styling advice for your man. That's "stylist," not "barber." Barbers are fine for kids and young guys who are into trendy barber-style buzzes. But when it's time for a grown-up haircut, it's time to find a stylist.

The problem is, how do you get your man to go see one, especially if he has a long-standing relationship with a barber or with another stylist who isn't doing right by him?

To begin with, don't criticize his hair.

"Men are very leery of being attacked for how they look because they know they can't groom as well as women," Johns says. "You're never going to make someone look better if you come from an attack space. You can't say to your man, 'Honey, your hair looks like shit.' "

Johns recommends that women use a more positive, indirect strategy. One way would be to try to get him to use *your* stylist, assuming that you're happy with that person. If so, a good, subtle icebreaker would be: "When I was at my hairdresser last week, he cut two men before me, and they looked so great. You have such beautiful hair—you should go talk to my guy."

If your man needs an even *more* subtle icebreaker, Johns suggests that you have him meet you at your stylist's the next time you have an appointment. ("Sweetie, pick me up at the salon at noon and then we can have lunch together.") Use the opportunity to introduce him casually to your stylist, who should be clued in to his hair situation. The two of them can chat, and your stylist can (hopefully) convince your man to come by for his next haircut.

Ideally, you will slip away during this conversation to pay the bill or use the ladies' room so that you're "out of the loop." This way, your man can talk to your stylist man-to-man (or man-to-professional, anyway), and there's no sense of you hanging around like his mommy and coercing him into "doing something about that awful hair!"

Still, that first visit to a new stylist may be really scary for your man, so "mother him without being his mother," suggests Johns. Ask him if he wants you to come with him. If he says yes, make the whole thing as pleasant, fun, and relaxing for him as possible. Says Johns: "Men are afraid no matter what age they are. They feel funny being groomed. The easier you can make that experience, the better."

To do this, you might offer your cheerful two cents when your stylist and your man are deliberating on a new do. Encourage your man to try something a little different: "Honey, why don't we make it less corporate and more beachy?" According to Johns, men often respond to that because they like the idea of looking like a "guy on a yacht" versus a "guy in a suit."

You can also be a helpmate to your man by clueing him in to tipping etiquette. He should tip the stylist like he would tip a good waiter: 15 to 20 percent. If the stylist owns the salon, don't tip. The shampoo person gets $3 to $5. If other people provide services for your man, they should be tipped, too.

The whole financial thing can be made even easier if you give your man a gift certificate for the whole package, including grooming products. ("Sweetie, your birthday's coming up, and I didn't know what to get you. I thought it might be fun for you to try my guy.")

Ultimately, it'll be up to your man if he wants to go back to your stylist for a second visit.

"If he doesn't want to go back, don't hound him," says Johns. "If he loves it, he'll tell you. If he doesn't, he'll tell you. It's his life and his hair."

Hair care 101

If you can fix your man up with a capable stylist, then he or she can suggest a hair care routine and the appropriate products for your man. But if you can't—maybe your man refuses to "break up" with his stylist who's stuck in early *Miami Vice* or his beloved old barber with the shaky hands—then try to encourage him to do *at least* the following:

- **Shampoo daily or so.** Your man should have several different shampoos on hand and switch back and forth between them every couple of weeks in order to avoid that build-up problem. Tempt him by buying him a couple of groovy-looking men's or unisex brands and leaving them lying around the bathroom. If your man has dandruff, he can use a dandruff shampoo such as Head & Shoulders or American Crew's Anti-Dandruff Shampoo—but he should switch back to a milder shampoo once the flakes are under control.

- **Condition after shampooing.** Men often skip this step, figuring that conditioning is another one of those "women's things." Again, buy him a men's conditioner and just kind of plant it in the shower caddy. After shampooing, he can apply the conditioner and leave it in for a few minutes while he's shaving, scrubbing, singing Sinatra tunes, or playing air guitar.

- **Blow-dry with care.** Your man should towel-dry his hair first, then blow-dry on the lowest setting possible. While his hair is still wet, he should de-tangle it with his fingers or a wide-toothed comb—not a brush, which can damage damp hair.

- **Gel, gel, gel.** Your man should be using gel (or pomade, or another hair-control product) to tame his unruly tresses and give shape to his style. Buy different types and brands and let him pick the one he likes best.

- **Be his personal shampoo girl.** If your man ignores all the products you buy for him and seems inclined to stick to his

How Often Should Your Man Get a Haircut?

Brad Johns says that your man's stylist is the best person to ask about this. A guy with super-short hair will probably have to go every two weeks. A guy with longer hair will have to go less often. At the end of his appointment, your man can ask his stylist when his *next* appointment should be and book it while he's thinking about it.

routine of washing his hair with a bar of Irish Spring, then it's time for some serious intervention. Tomorrow morning, get in the shower with him. Say, "Honey, let *me* do that for you," and wash his hair for him—with the good stuff. Follow up with conditioner and then a blow-drying session. After a few days of this, see if he doesn't catch on.

When there's not as much up there as there used to be

Does your man suffer from *androgenetic alopecia*? Sounds scary, doesn't it? It's more commonly known by the name male pattern baldness (although it can affect us ladies, too).

You may think that your man's shiny dome is sexy—so Yul Brenner, so Sean Connery, so Michael Jordan! (If so, make sure to tell him so.) Or you may wish he had his lush mop of blond curls back. Or you may not care either way, but your honey does.

There are only two hair-loss treatments on the market that have FDA approval: minoxidil (Rogaine) and finasteride (Propecia). However, there are a number of side-effect, safety, and effectiveness issues with both. If your man is interested in pursuing

Don't Try This at Home

If your man wants to downplay his distinguished gray or otherwise play around with his hair color, encourage him to see an experienced colorist—not do it himself at home. According to colorist Brad Johns, highlights will probably require two or more visits a year. More serious permanent color may require a visit every three weeks.

the pharmaceutical route, he should discuss his options thoroughly with his doctor or dermatologist.

Herbs promoted as hair-loss treatments include the saw palmetto, maidenhair fern, and horsetail plant. However, there are no studies to support their effectiveness. There are a number of other products, from wheat germ oil to "revitalizing systems" to special combs, that also claim to promote hair growth—but again, there are no supporting studies.

Remember: Your man can do a lot with a little! A good stylist can work with what hair he *does* have and give him a flattering cut. Or your man could elect to "shave it all off."

But under no circumstances should your man "comb it over."

For more information, your man could check out several websites devoted to the topic: www.hairlosstalk.com, www.regrowth.com, and www.thebaldtruth.com.

Taking care of his hands and nails

In D. H. Lawrence's novel *Lady Chatterley's Lover*, the elegant lady of the estate was seduced by Oliver Mellors, the gardener. Great stuff! But while the idea of being given the once-over by a working man's rough, callused hands sounds incredibly *appealing*, the reality doesn't quite match up.

"Hank is a mechanic, and he doesn't wear gloves when he works, so his hands get all dry and coarse," says Joanne, age 32. "When he touches me, it feels like sandpaper!"

And there is the issue of nails. "Dale bites his nails, so they look ragged and god-awful," 39-year-old Luanne complains. "When he *does* trim them, he does it on the couch while he's watching TV, and the nail clippings go flying all over the place. Yuck!"

As with other aspects of grooming, men don't like the idea of "fussing" with their hands and nails. Some men can get away with a minimum of care, but others aren't so fortunate—or careful.

Hand and nail maintenance doesn't take a lot of effort. If you can't convince your honey to get a professional manicure—and you probably won't be able to, unless he knows other guys who do it—then offer to give him one at home. Tell him that you find well-groomed nails sexy. Tell him they'll go better with his Rolex (or Timex). Tell him that you love the idea of being caressed by his baby-smooth hands.

For a basic at-home manicure:

- Clean any dirt from under your man's nails. Be very gentle, and don't go too far in.

- Clip your man's nails with one of those small nail clippers you can get at any drugstore. Clip the center of the nail first, then do the sides. Don't clip the whole nail at once.

- File your man's nails with an emery board (not one of those metal files). File in one direction only, or you might cause splits.

• Put some cream or lotion on your man's hands and give them a nice, slow, luxurious massage. Your man has been typing away on his computer or pounding nails all day, and his hands are *soooooo* tired.

• Soak your man's hands in a bowl of warm water with a bit of bubble bath and a drop of scented oil in it. While he's soaking, rub his shoulders. Mmmmmm.

• Finally, push back his cuticles gently. You can use a Q-tip, an orange stick wrapped with cotton, or a soft washcloth. Don't use anything sharp, like a nail file or your own fingernails. And most important, don't cut them!

Ta-da! Otherwise, encourage your man to keep his hands and nails extra-smooth by moisturizing often (make sure he has a bottle of hand cream or lotion on his side of the nightstand and in the bathroom—and maybe try to sneak one into his gym bag, too). Ideally, he should also wear rubber gloves when he washes the dishes or performs other hand-unfriendly chores. Leave a pair lying next to the kitchen sink and see if he catches on.

Taking care of his feet

What is it with men and their long, long, *long* toenails? I've heard so many women complain about being stabbed in the middle of the night by their men's lethal piggies.

"My wife doesn't like my toenails," confessed Jonah, who's 54. "She says they're too long. In bed, she'll just yell, 'Get those out of there!' "

I asked him why he didn't just cut them. He just shrugged and looked at me with a confused face.

Men!

I then asked him if a possible solution might be for his wife to give him a relaxing pedicure. He stopped shrugging, and his eyes grew enormous. "I would *love* a pedicure," he sighed dreamily.

Okay, ladies.

To give your man a pedicure:

• Soak your man's feet in a big pan full of warm water with a little baby oil mixed in.

• After drying them off, give them a massage. Make slow, circular motions up and down each foot with your thumb. Rub those piggies one by one. Knead each foot as if it were bread dough. Finish off with light, caressing strokes.

• Slough off dead skin with an exfoliating foot peel (available at drugstores).

• Trim your man's toenails with clippers. Cut them straight across—don't cut the corners.

• File the edges lightly with an emery board.

• Finish off with a light moisturizer.

In addition to keeping those toenails clipped (whether by you or by himself), your man should remember the following foot care guidelines:

• He should use a pumice stone to slough off dead skin whenever he takes a shower.

• He should put lotion on his feet after bathing.

• To avoid foot odor, he should stick to shoes and socks made of natural materials (leather and canvas for shoes, cotton for socks). He should also rotate his shoes every day to let them dry out. When he's not wearing them, they should be airing on a wooden shoe rack.

• To avoid athlete's foot, your man should wear flip-flops or other waterproof sandals when showering at the gym.

• It's crucially important that he get shoes that fit. Otherwise, he will find himself with blisters, bunions, corns, calluses, and more.

• If your man is suffering from an ingrown toenail, try the following. First, soak his foot in warm water. Then pull back the skin at the side of the toenail ever so gently. Lift the nail (again, ever so gently) and place a piece of dental floss under it to separate the nail from the irritated skin. Do this every day until the nail grows out. If this doesn't take care of it, your man may need to see his doctor or a podiatrist.

Taking care of his mouth and teeth

Rachel, 44, has no issues with husband Anthony's grooming habits—except when it comes to his teeth.

"He doesn't go to the dentist! He doesn't want to schedule it around work," she said.

"I think my boyfriend flosses about once a month. He doesn't think it's important," was the complaint of 23-year-old Helena.

"Bad breath!" said several women of their men.

Okay. First of all, your man has to go to the dentist—twice a year, just like everyone else. Schedule those appointments for him if necessary. If the dentist's hours aren't convenient for his work schedule, find one with evening or weekend hours.

Convince your man that there is nothing sexy about yellow, chipped, cavity-filled, rotting teeth. And hit him in the other place that hurts—his pocket. Because if he wants to keep up his poor dental hygiene, he might as well start liquidating some mutual funds right now to pay for the exorbitant oral surgery he'll have to get down the line.

Here are the basics:

• Your man should floss every day. Get him some cinnamon- or mint-flavored floss, if that will make it more enticing for him. Explain to him (in your best mean-but-sexy nurse voice) that if he doesn't floss daily, the tiny, itty-bitty food particles that get stuck between his teeth will quickly morph into cavity-causing bacteria.

• When it comes to brushing, your man should use a tooth-brush with soft bristles—not hard ones, which can be irritating.

• Rinsing with mouthwash is his call. It doesn't do a whole lot to help the bacteria-killing process, but it does do *something*— and it might make his mouth feel all minty and nice.

• If your man smokes—and he shouldn't!—he really needs to push the oral hygiene. The heat from cigarettes can damage gums. The tar and nicotine create a drekky film in his mouth that encourages growth of bacteria. Plus, his kisses will taste yucky unless he's constantly brushing, flossing, and rinsing.

As for bad breath: If you suspect that your man's bad breath might be caused by a medical issue such as gingivitis or a sinus infection, make an appointment for him to see his dentist or doc-

Mars and Venus practice Oral Hygiene

According to an American Academy of Periodontology survey of 2,001 periodontists, female patients practiced better oral hygiene than male ones. The most common excuses for not flossing? Lack of time and "dexterity problems." Better get your men to work on that wrist action, ladies.

tor. Otherwise, good oral hygiene is the key. Your man should also remember to brush his tongue (or scrape it with a tongue scraper or piece of silverware) whenever he brushes his teeth, since bacteria can grow on the tongue and emit an odor.

Finally, awareness is everything. "I started brushing my teeth after every meal and popping Altoids a lot," said 28-year-old Althea. "I told my boyfriend I was doing that because I wanted to be super-kissable for him. He got the hint and started doing it, too."

Taking care of his facial hair

"He shaves carelessly (bloodily). I wish I didn't have blood-stains on my pillowcases from when he shaves at night," said 40-year-old Katie of husband, Reg.

"He thinks the short stubble thing is sexy. It's not only un-sexy, it hurts my face when I kiss him!" said 27-year-old Natasha of her boyfriend, Patrick.

Your man is a man, which probably means that he learned how to shave when he was a teenager and has been doing it that way pretty much since then.

But maybe he never learned to do it quite right. Or maybe he thinks his facial hair (whether it's stubble, a mustache, a goatee, or a beard) is just fine as it is—and you beg to differ.

To begin with, here are some shaving basics your man should know:

• To prevent bloody pillowcases and the like, your man should be shaving in the morning. His skin is less sensitive then.

• He should soak his skin for several minutes in warm water first. He can do this by splashing his face; applying a warm, wet towel; or best of all, shaving in the shower.

• Encourage your man to use shaving gel or cream, not just plain old soap. He should leave the lather on for a few minutes before putting blade to beard.

• Your man should not be using a blade or disposable razor past its lifespan, of which only he can be the real judge. (To help in this department, buy him a lot of refills so he's not always running out.)

• Your man should shave in the same direction as his facial hairs grow.

• Your man may suffer from *pseudofolliculitis barbae*—a.k.a. razor bumps—a.k.a. he shaved too closely, so the hairs grew back into his skin and caused inflammation and infection. This condition is especially common with African-American men. One solution is a topical treatment product containing liquid aspirin. (Ask your man's dermatologist.) But prevention is the best medicine. Make sure your man follows the above-mentioned shaving guidelines—and in addition, he should not pull his skin tightly across his face in order to get a closer shave.

If you are not happy with your man's choice of facial hair-style—i.e., George Clooney stubble, mustache, goatee, or beard—you have several options. You could just be honest with him and tell him you liked him better with a smooth face. You could shave him while he's asleep. (Just kidding. Or maybe not.)

Or you could try what Miranda, 27, did with her husband, Garrett:

> *He had this idea for a while that he was going to grow a goatee. I hated that thing. We fought a lot. He said I was being bitchy and controlling. I said I didn't control anything in his life (I don't too much!), but I hated the goatee. I refused to have sex with him until he shaved it. It worked—he hasn't tried to grow one in more than a year now.*

Taking care of unwanted body hair

Fifty-four-year-old Jonah says that sometimes his wife will just come at him with a pair of scissors. "This is really bugging me," she'll announce, and before he can react, she'll clip an extra-long nose hair.

Ann, 38, tried a similar solution with her man's extra-bushy eyebrows:

> *I used to go out with this guy. He was pretty well-groomed, but his eyebrows were totally overgrown. I didn't say anything at first, but then I did.*
>
> *I just said, "You have some eyebrows that are really out of control." He said, "Oh, really?" Then he looked in the mirror*

*and realized that I was telling the truth. I said, "I could trim
them for you."*

*So I started grooming his eyebrows for him. I did this every
month. He would put his head down, I'd rub his temples, and
I'd do his eyebrows for him. I would pluck a couple of hairs
out. I would trim them with little scissors. He loved having me
touch his face. He loved the attention.*

Nose hair, ear hair, and caveman eyebrows are among our
men's biggest problems when it comes to unwanted body hair.

With nose and ear hairs: Your man (or you) should be trim-
ming them regularly. Don't use scissors, because accidental cuts
can happen. Electric snippers or razors are best.

Eyebrow tweezing is done best after a shower, when pores are
open. Use angled tweezers and remove only the longest, most offensive hairs. Proceed slowly and carefully, and do one brow at a time,
so you (or your man) can see the difference between the two brows.
Pluck only about a half-an-inch of hair between the eyebrows.

Chest hair and back hair can be shaved or waxed. Which re-
minds me—at his wife's request, a friend of mine recently shaved
his chest. Apparently his wife bragged about this at a party, because when he walked into the room, no less than 15 women
rushed up to him and asked him to take his shirt off so they could
"touch it."

If you want your man to shave his chest, you might share that
story with him.

Deodorants, antiperspirants, colognes, and aftershaves

There can be something wonderful—*wonderful*—about the natural smell of a man's skin.

But in most cases, your man can probably benefit from deodorant or an antiperspirant.

In case you haven't figured it out yet, there *is* a difference between the two products. Deodorants cover up body odor. Antiperspirants actually keep the sweat from coming out of your man's pores. There are a number of products on the market that are a combination of the two.

"Deodorants make Derek break out so he doesn't use it," says 42-year-old Sally of her husband. "This is sometimes annoying, but he won't try new or natural brands. On the other hand, he showers once or twice a day."

If your man is allergic, like Derek, he might try a "crystal," which can often be found at health-food stores. These crystals act as an antiperspirant (but not as a deodorant) without the usual fragrances and preservatives that are characteristic of antiperspirant products. If your man is even allergic to crystals, he might try baking soda or powder, which can absorb wetness.

When it comes to colognes and aftershaves: I've found in my limited experience that these are highly personal items for men. There are men who like fragrance products, and men who just don't.

Colognes are stronger than aftershaves. Aftershaves contain a great deal of alcohol and can cause a stinging sensation to your man's skin after he shaves. He might prefer to use a scented moisturizer instead.

As you may know from wearing your own fragrance, it can be

Does Your Man Sweat Too Much?

If your man has an excessive sweating problem, antiperspirants and deodorants probably won't do the trick. Endocrine disorders such as an overactive thyroid, certain cancers, chronic infections, and other illnesses can cause people to "sweat buckets," forcing them to shower and change clothes many times a day. Or there may a more innocuous underlying cause, such as an overreaction to spicy foods.

In any case, your man should get checked out by your family doctor to rule out a medical condition. There are prescription medications—both oral and topical—that may help. Surgery may also be an option.

difficult to know how much is too much. You can help your man learn how much cologne or aftershave to put on. Have him apply some to pulse points such as his neck, wrist, and chest. After a few minutes, stand several feet away from him—and sniff. His fragrance should not be detectable unless you're very close to him, and it shouldn't hang in the air. (By the way, he should never wear fragrance at the gym—it will combine with his sweat and get very funky and offensive.)

If your man doesn't wear a fragrance but you think he might be open to trying one, take him shopping! Get a bunch of samples at a department store of scents that appeal to both of you, go home, and have him try one sample on each evening before he goes to bed. Let the scent mingle with your man's natural chemistry over the course of the night. In the morning, play scratch-and-sniff games before he showers off the scent. When the two of you decide on the one that's *him*, go back to the store and buy him a bottle.

Another way to get him interested in fragrance is to buy a bottle—and wear it yourself. Preferably with nothing else.

Chapter Seven

"It's the latest version of the stress test. We'll monitor your heart rate as you try to feed these seven hungry babies with just one bottle."

Relaxing Your Man

Tara, 32, worries that her boyfriend, Steven's, long hours and stress level are chipping away at his health, his overall mood, and his boyish good looks:

He works in a high-power law firm, so he comes home most days at 8 or 9 P.M. Then he'll read briefs or make overseas calls till 10 or 11. By the time he's ready for bed he's really tense and wound up. He usually needs a Scotch to fall asleep. In the middle of the night, I hear him tossing and turning and getting up a lot.

Stress is *not* your man's friend. Stress can increase his risk for a host of health problems, including heart disease, stroke, diabetes, ulcers, irritable bowel syndrome, and more. It can lead to depression. It can lower his immunity. It can put a dent in his energy level. It can put a dent in his sex drive. And on and on.

All of which will keep him from looking and feeling his very best. Because a guy who is on a low simmer all day at work, then comes home to simmer some more, is probably hitting the junk food or the booze, and not taking care of himself in a hundred other ways.

Helping your man unwind after a long day—and giving him the tools to decompress while he's on his own—will go a long way toward keeping him happy, healthy, and gorgeous.

Stress-busting basics

To begin with, here are some sure-fire tips for beating stress. Help your man make them a part of his daily routine—starting today:

- **Exercise!** A regular exercise program is one of the best ways to relieve stress. Going for a jog in the morning or hitting the gym at lunchtime will help your man take his mind off of job pressures, money pressures, and other pressures, too. Also, after about half an hour of aerobic exercise, he will experience a "runner's high"—that wonderful, calm feeling caused by a release of endorphins in his brain—that will linger long after his workout is over.

- **Breathe.** Just the act of taking a big, deep breath can relax your man. (Go ahead, do it yourself *right now*—you'll see what I mean.) To help him remember, put little Post-it notes on his desk at work, on his favorite seat at home, and on the dashboard of his car reading: BREATHE. (Hearts and smiley faces optional.)

- **Take breaks.** It's important to indulge in little mental health breaks throughout the day. Encourage your man to take a walk around the block, take a walk to the drinking fountain and back, get up to do some stretches, or just close the door and be alone with his thoughts whenever he needs to "take a time out."

• **Disconnect.** In this age of cell phones, pagers, e-mail, and voicemail, it seems almost impossible to get away. Your man should get in the habit of checking messages only when necessary and allotting specific chunks of time to return calls and e-mails. Otherwise, the nonstop ringing of the phone and the endless siren song of "You've got mail!!!" will only add another layer of craziness to his day.

• **Organize.** Each night, help your man organize his thoughts and his To-Do list for the following day. He needs to feel that "it's under control" so he can leave it behind, unwind, and know that he'll be able to hit the ground running in the morning.

• **Let him lean on you.** Tell your man to call you—or call *on* you—whenever he needs to vent, blow off steam, whine, complain, or scream—even for half a minute. Just having a loving, sympathetic voice who will side with him no matter what can take the edge off his escalating stress.

With some or all of these suggestions, you can either adopt a direct, "Why don't you . . ." approach with your man—or you can be more indirect and subtle, telling your man that these are some things you've been doing to deal with your *own* stress. Whatever works.

Massage his cares away

For some people, the word *massage* is synonymous with "relaxation." Therapeutic massage is an age-old remedy for melting away cares, turning tight muscles into Jell-O, and making a person feel that all is right with the world.

In addition to all this warm, fuzzy, noodly stuff, massage boasts an impressive range of health benefits. Among other things, it can relieve headaches and backaches, alleviate anxiety, improve the circulatory and immune systems, and speed post-exercise recovery.

If your man has never had a professional massage, you might consider giving him a gift certificate for a half-hour or hour-long session. Look up "massage" or "therapeutic massage" in the Yellow Pages—or better yet, get a referral from your family doctor, a massage-savvy friend, or even your local gym.

Your man may be skittish about his first massage because he doesn't know what to expect. Here are some basics that might help put him at ease:

• Before the session, your man's massage therapist will want to know why he has come for a massage ("My back's killing me"; "I've been doing too many squats at the gym"; "My girlfriend made me"), as well as any relevant information about your man's physical condition. This way, the massage therapist will be able to tailor the session to his needs.

• For the session itself, your man will probably be draped with a large towel or sheet. He can choose to be totally or partially naked under the drape. Many people prefer to leave their underpants on during a massage. Some types of massage, such as shiatsu (pressure-point massage), can be performed while your man is fully clothed in comfortable clothing.

• Your man can choose to talk or not during his massage. Some people prefer silence; some people prefer to make conversation. Either way, if he is uncomfortable at any time—e.g., if a massage stroke is too deep or painful—he should let his massage therapist know right away.

• The massage therapist will probably use oil, lotion, or another lubricant so his or her hands will slide over your man's skin without pulling or chaffing. Your man should let the massage therapist know if he has any allergies to such products.

• And finally: Remember that episode of *Seinfeld* where George was afraid to get a professional massage because "it" might "move" during the session? If your man has the same fear, tell him to think about baseball or tax receipts during the session. Or you could make a point of scheduling his appointment with a massage therapist whom your man is not likely to find terribly attractive.

You can also learn to give your man massages at home. A quick mini-massage, focusing on a specific part of his body, can be super-relaxing: a hand massage, a foot massage, a shoulder massage, or a temple massage. You can use scented or unscented lotion or oil, or nothing at all. Remember to use slow, lingering strokes, and don't rub too hard or deep (unless your man requests it).

For an extra-special treat, give your man a full-body massage. Get some books or videos on the subject and teach yourself the basic strokes. Remember to make the massage extra-relaxing for him with soft music and scented candles.

Note: Massage is primarily about nonsexual touch and relaxation. Part of why it's so great for your man to receive a massage from you is that he can really float away, mentally and physically, without having to worry about "performing" sexually.

That being said: Massage can be a wonderful part of, or prelude to, sexual intimacy. For some inspiration and instruction on how to stroke your man into a state of total bliss, get a copy of *Erotic Massage: The Tantric Touch of Love* by Kenneth Ray Stubbs.

Yoga for two

Yoga has long been acknowledged as a way to de-stress, build strength, enhance breathing, increase flexibility, and get in touch with our emotional and spiritual selves. Its popularity has exploded in the last decade or so as people stopped perceiving it as some sort of "out-there" mystical experience for vegetarians and Buddhists, and started embracing it as a valuable practice for everyday life. These days, athletes, corporate executives, Hollywood celebrities, and others are flocking to yoga classes in droves or doing yoga at home with books and videos.

And then there's partner yoga.

Partner yoga is an interactive form of yoga that involves two people doing yoga postures together. The postures, which are also done in solo yoga, can be made easier by having a partner to hold you up, balance you, twist you, and bend you.

But the act of doing postures with a partner has another, more emotional side to it, too.

"Partner yoga emphasizes how you communicate—or don't communicate—with your partner," says Anne Greene, who co-teaches partner yoga and other yoga classes with her husband, Todd Norian, at the Kripalu Institute in Lenox, Massachusetts, and elsewhere. "You find out that you don't tell your partner what you need. You fall over because you didn't stand your ground. Metaphors will come up that will mirror aspects of your relationship, of your life, of how you live day to day."

Two people can come into a partner yoga class with serious "issues"—and leave with a fresh new perspective. "Once you touch each other and breathe together, you come together," says Greene. "It's very primal."

"It also helps two people become more respectful of each other," adds Norian.

And cooperative. "You have to work together to construct the postures," says Greene.

The postures have poetic names such as the "Warrior," the "Camel," the "Lord of the Fishes," and the "Standing Tree." Often, people who cannot do the postures effectively on their own can do them with the help of a partner. (A wonderful metaphor for relationships!)

Greene and Norian say that they are beginning to see more and more men in *all* their yoga classes. "Men are more into yoga now," Greene acknowledges. "All these women who have been doing it for years and years are finally getting their husbands interested in it."

You can check out Greene and Norian's partner yoga video—and also get information on their classes—at their website, www.deeppeaceyoga.com. There is also a terrific book on the subject: *Partner Yoga: Making Contact for Physical, Emotional, and Spiritual Growth* by Cain Carroll, Lori Kimata, and Peter J. D'Adamo. Or call your local yoga center to see about classes. Previous experience is not necessary—according to Greene and Norian, beginners can jump right into partner yoga.

Meditation

Meditation is another practice that people used to associate with vegetarians and Buddhists. Now, it is embraced as a terrific way for "regular folks" to relax, focus, take a break from the real world, or just take a break.

In its simplest form, meditation can be about unplugging the phone, locking the door, closing your eyes, and focusing on your breathing. *In . . . out . . . in . . . out . . .* chasing all other thoughts from your mind, all that "Did I remember to call the sitter?" and "Am I ever going to get that report done in time?" stuff, and just concentrating on the rhythm and sensation of breathing.

If you think your man can sit still for long enough, encourage him to meditate with you once a day. Early morning is best, although nighttime can be great, too.

Make sure the two of you are wearing comfortable clothing (or none at all). Sit cross-legged or with your legs in front of you and your backs against a wall. (Lying down can also work, although it may make you sleepy.)

During the meditation session, annoying thoughts may pop into your head. If this happens, just slowly and calmly return your focus to your breathing. It can also help to repeat the phrase "Let it go" to re-empty the mind.

Meditate for 5 minutes, 10 minutes, half an hour—whatever feels comfortable.

You and your man can also consider taking a meditation class. If he's reluctant, tell him that practicing meditation will help his mental focus and give him an edge at work.

Relaxation in a bottle

No, not *that* kind of a bottle. One terrific way to help your man unwind is with aromatherapy.

Aromatherapy is the use of essential plant oils to promote wellness. Oils such as lavender, rose, peppermint, and juniper can be inhaled, applied to the skin, or used in a bath in order to induce relaxation, heightened energy, relief from a cold, and more.

In her wonderful book *Mary Lee's Natural Health and Beauty: Healthy Living with Essential Oils*, author Mary Lee Patton recommends the following essential oils for relieving stress:

- Bergamot
- Cedarwood
- Chamomile
- Cinnamon
- Clove
- Frankincense
- Geranium
- Ginger
- Grapefruit
- Jasmine
- Lavender
- Lemon
- Neroli
- Orange
- Petitgrain
- Rose
- Sandalwood
- Ylang ylang

You can use these oils to relax your man in a number of ways. Put a few drops into or onto:

- His handkerchief.

- A diffuser lightbulb ring, which can be purchased at natural health stores and companies specializing in essential oils and aromatherapy products.

- An aromatherapy clay pot (same sources as above).

- A humidifier or vaporizer.

• Your man's massage lotion or oil.

• Your man's bath.

Make sure you purchase the essential oils from a reliable source, like a health-food store or spa setting. (Patton has a wonderful company, Earth Tribe, which sells essential oils, blends, and other feel-good products. Check out her website at www.earthtribe.com.)

Give your man sweet dreams

We are a seriously sleep-deprived nation. With jobs, families, and other 24/7 demands, it seems as though sleep is often the first thing to go. Most experts agree that adults need eight hours of sleep per night—but many settle for seven or even six.

Your man's health, wellness, and good looks are going to be seriously affected if he is living on less than eight hours of sleep each night, if he has a hard time falling asleep, or if he does a lot of tossing, turning, and getting up during the wee hours. Sleep deprivation can impair his alertness, reaction time, memory, patience, productivity at work—and even his relationship with you.

Here are some tips to help him get the zzzzz's he needs:

• Try to get him to go to sleep at the same time every night. He shouldn't stay up late or sleep in on weekends or he'll get "Sunday-night insomnia."

• Establish a regular, hour-long "wind-down" routine that will make your man want to come to bed. Light pretty candles in your bedroom and bathroom. Take a bath together (with

Does Your Man Snore?

If your man snores, he should try sleeping on his side, using a humidifier, and avoiding alcohol, snacks, sleeping pills, and antihistamines several hours before bedtime. If he is overweight, that might be a contributing factor. He should also get his blood pressure checked—a recent study suggests a link between high blood pressure and sleep problems such as snoring. He should also rule out sleep apnea, a condition that keeps people from breathing properly during sleep. Beware of so-called "anti-snoring" devices such as jaw retainers and contoured pillows, none of which have been scientifically proven to work. If your man's snoring is caused by certain types of nasal obstruction, his doctor may recommend a type of nasal dilator called Breathe Right, which has been approved by the FDA.

lavender salts and oil). Give him a massage. Have a coed naked yoga session. Read poetry to each other by candlelight.

• Discourage your man from taking long naps during the day, which can keep him from falling asleep at night. However, a daily 20- or 30-minute "power nap" in the middle of the afternoon can have a beneficial, rejuvenating effect.

• Your man should avoid snacks a few hours before bedtime.

• Discourage him from having an alcoholic nightcap, which can wake him up in the middle of the night.

• Give your man a glass of warm milk; tryptophan is a natural sleep-inducer.

• Make a rule: The bed is only for sleeping, reading, and cuddling. It is not for working, TV-watching, or fighting about bills.

• Assess the physical environment of your bedroom. Is your mattress comfortable? (If not, consider investing in a better one.) Is the room too hot or too cold? (If so, adjust as necessary.) Do street sounds or noisy neighbors keep you or your man up? (If so, consider earplugs, a white noise machine, double-pane windows, heavy drapes, or a nasty note to the neighbors.)

• Put a few drops of lavender oil on his pillow.

• Encourage him to exercise every day. Working out in the afternoon can be particularly helpful for getting a good night's sleep.

• If your man can't fall asleep after 15 minutes, he should get up and do something else, then return to bed when he is tired. He should not let himself stew about the fact that he can't fall asleep—the stress will only exacerbate the problem.

• If your man's insomnia or other sleep problems don't seem to be going away, make an appointment with his doctor.

Chapter Eight

© 1993 John McPherson/Distributed by Universal Press Syndicate

McPHERSON   8-9

**Helen tries out her new
"Not-Tonight-Honey" nightgown.**

"No Sex Until…" and Other Tips
from the Home Front

Necessity is the mother of invention, and women everywhere seem to have invented creative ways to tweak their men's appearance in one direction or the other. No doubt our men are doing the same with us. (And exchanging tips over a round of pints somewhere—"Hey, Joe, your wife ever forget to wear deodorant?" "I finally got mine to join the gym." "Jeez Louise, mine can't seem to put her eyeshadow on straight!")

Here are some strategies that have worked for other women with their husbands and boyfriends. I hope they will inspire you in your quest to help your man look good:

Start with sweet-talk . . . then manipulate . . . then threaten: "No sex until . . ." (Joanne, 46, married 22 years)

When he's dressing, I say, "That works okay . . ." leaving the "but" silent, then adding, "What about this shirt, do you like it? How about this tie instead" (and I sweeten it with something appropriate like, "It's the one Paul and Jane gave you" or "You look so great in this"). (Victoria, 42, married 6 years)

I try to think about how I'd want him to tell me if my outfit didn't work. (Taylor, 22, married 1 year)

He finally started going to the gym. I tell him all the time how hot he looks, since he started working out. It motivates him! (Beth, 32, with boyfriend 3 years)

Sometimes I have to throw out something he has worn to death. (Catherine, 66, married 47 years)

I got him to join a club with me and we did aerobics together for a couple of years. We also used to run together before my knees gave out. Now we Rollerblade. (Susana, 44, married 3 years)

I try to focus on my own appearance and not on his. He is his own man. But I have to admit that I was glad when he started picking up some of my healthy habits, like eating oatmeal for breakfast or running on weekends. It's nice that I can inspire him that way. (Gail, 34, living with boyfriend 5 years)

He had to come to his own conclusions about what he wore and how he looked. I couldn't just snap and tell him, "Change that shirt." As long as he made the decisions—and I just commented—he'd come to his senses and throw out his terrible old hats, shirts, and pants. (Miranda, 27, married 4 years)

I try to be as direct as possible without being negative or hurting his feelings. (Katie, 40, married 5 years)

I suggest something and then when he does it, or wears it, I compliment him mercilessly! If he puts on something I think is bad news, or refuses to wash his hair when it looks really dirty, I groan about it, and he usually comes around. (Lisa, with boyfriend 1 year)

I reinforce it as much as I can. Whenever he makes himself a healthy meal or goes to the gym, I tell him what a great example he's setting for the kids. (Rita, 35, married 8 years)

I buy him clothes every chance I get . . . but I don't make a big deal out of it. I'll come home and say, "I saw this shirt at The Gap, I thought this blue would look so sexy with your eyes." He loves the attention. (Kara, 31, living with boyfriend 2 years)

I think helping a man look good goes beyond appearance. Can you help him find himself? Can you help him realize happiness? Without happiness or peace he will not look good. (Rachel, 44, married 22 years)

I tell him that "I'd get turned on if . . ." (Kristin, 38, living with boyfriend 1 year)

Remarkably, his friends have had the best impact. Hal chose a new razor and shaving regimen based on one man's advice. And ever since that friend turned him on to some new habits, he uses a weekly facial scrub, a scented moisturizer I bought for him, a triple-blade razor, and an aftershave balm instead of an alcohol-based cologne. He now goes to my haircutter because he found out that another man whose good grooming he admires goes to her as well. (Victoria, 42, married 6 years)

I don't care about the clothes or the colognes or anything. But I do care about his health. If he starts eating badly and gaining *a lot of weight, I tell him honestly, "If you keep that up, I'm so scared you're going to have a heart attack like your dad."* (Audrey, 45, married 16 years)

Encourage the best with a positive outlook. Don't see the worst, and don't be critical and hurtful. They have big egos and are sensitive. (Margaret, 51, married 30 years)

I buy new shirts for him and he appreciates it. (Wendy, 51, married 25 years)

He had a pair of brown polyester shorts that he made by cutting an old leisure suit. I hated those and threatened to throw them away, much to his dismay. I hid them in his closet and he never found them. (Susana, 44, married 3 years)

I compare him to other men. (Danielle, 42, married 19 years)

One day I just went through his closet and threw half the stuff out. I never told him, and he never noticed. (Ingrid, 35, married 12 years)

I buy 95 percent of his clothes. (Martha, 42, married 26 years)

He's impervious to all external influences except his mother, whom he tries to look good for. (Helena, 46, married 13 years)

Don't nag. (Wendy, 51, married 25 years)

I think people look best when they feel confident and loved. If you respect their differences and allow them to be who they are, they will look better. (Rachel, 44, married 22 years)

I make it part of the sexual game and he responds very well—except when I want to trim his toenails. (Victoria, 42, married 6 years)

I'm honest but still manipulative. I will say, "I don't think that looks right." Then I don't say anything else. He'll huff and puff about it for a while. (By stomping around the house and grumbling, "You think you know everything.") But then if I sit back and let him stew, he'll change his appearance. He'll shave, change the shirt, put on different pants. (Miranda, 27, married 4 years)

The only way to talk to him about changing his appearance is to get him drunk (I mean, "in a good mood"). Or I will buy something that I like and ask him to try it. (Juliana, 37, married 13 years)

I think the key to "making over" your special someone is not to try and change them but encourage them to take risks and give them the confidence to believe they can look good many different ways. (Anna, 34, married 1 year)

Never point to his wealthy and well-dressed friends for comparison—he'll do it himself, eventually. (Victoria, 42, married 6 years)

Bribe them! Whatever works—usually sex. Sex usually works with men. (Ann, 38, married 1 year)

Sex, sex, and more sex

That word sure seems to come up a lot, doesn't it?

The sex card is used by women to improve their man's appearance, whether it's promising more of it, threatening less of it, or creating a general aura of sexiness and sexuality that makes a man more . . . well, *agreeable.* Is it manipulative? Maybe. Does it work? Definitely.

Of course, there's another side to the issue. If your man looks his best, he's likely to be more attractive to you . . . and you're likely to want to get cuddly with him more often.

"He is definitely more attractive to me when he dresses well and when he wears Versace Dreamer," said one woman of her husband.

Conversely, if your man *doesn't* look so great, you may be pleading headaches a lot. One woman complained: "My husband gets a homeless look going, which I am *not attracted to.*"

And there are the in-between cases, like one woman who said of her husband, "I am always attracted to him, except when he wears sweat pants out of the house."

Ultimately, it *can* be a win-win for everyone. If more sex means your honey sheds the pounds, the long toenails, or the bad wardrobe, you will be happier—and he will look and feel a whole lot better. Which will lead to more sex. Which will lead to the two of you being even happier. How can you argue with that?

Tough nuts

But what if even *sex* doesn't work with your man?

There are some guys out there who seem immune to any and

all appeals in the appearance department. Sex doesn't work. Compliments don't work. Little hints don't work. Big hints *definitely* don't work.

And gifts of clothes, grooming products, and gym memberships just sit gathering dust in his closet (behind the sneakers with the holes and under the avocado-green leisure suit with the sangria stains).

If your man is a tough nut—if you've tried all the positive, nurturing strategies in this book, with zero results (except maybe more aggravation for you)—then consider the following:

• Can you learn to live with his imperfections, whether it's serious love handles or hair like Chewbacca? Focus on his good points. Realize that once you stop spinning your wheels about his shortcomings, you'll free up a lot of time and energy for yourself.

• Was he like this when you first met him? If so, why are you trying to change him now? It's one thing if your man is open to change on some level, and it's just a matter of getting him there. But if your man has a DO NOT DISTURB sign posted on his mind, his closet door, and his bathroom mirror, you may just have to make your peace with that.

• Is there something deeper going on, whether in him or in your relationship? Is your man depressed, angry, passive-aggressive—or all of the above? Have the two of you been tap-dancing around a major relationship rift for a long time? Take a long, hard look at him—and at the two of you as a couple—and see if counseling might not be in order. If he won't go, go alone.

But what if *you're* the tough nut?

"I don't get it," said one woman. "Why would you *want* your man to look good? If he looks *too* good, he might get ideas and leave you for somebody else."

Like this woman, you may have mixed feelings about the prospect of your man getting thinner, buffer, and better-dressed—because with it comes the potential for more sexual attention from other women. It's like the line in the Bonnie Raitt–Sippie Wallace duet, "Women Be Wise": "Don't advertise your man!"

On the other hand, you might feel perfectly fine about other ladies checking out your man. As one woman said, "Some women probably feel flattered when their man looks good and other women are looking at him. They say to themselves: 'Yup, he's sexy, but he's mine!' "

It's a complicated issue that goes to the messy, muddled heart of love, commitment, and "happily ever after." When it comes right down to it, how secure are you with the relationship? How secure is he? How secure are the two of you with yourselves?

"But I'm fine with him the way he is," you might insist. "I don't care if he's a little hefty. I don't care if his clothes look a little beat-up."

That's great. But is *he* fine with the way he is? If deep down in your gut you know that your guy needs to lose weight (because it just isn't healthy) or update his wardrobe (because he'll have a better chance of getting promoted), you need to bite the bullet, put aside your insecurities, and help him get there.

And if you *do* help him get there, you will probably have one grateful, devoted guy on your hands for the rest of your life.

"I'm sorry, Mr. Credley, but due to our new truth-in-advertising policy, your request for a vanity plate reading 'BUFF-HUNK' has been denied."

Stand by Your Man

Remember Cheryl and her ex-husband, Dan, the serial clothes-stapler? The one she went on a shopping spree for before allowing him to meet her parents? After four years of being divorced, they are seeing each other again. She says that after the initial "dramatic improvement" in his clothing style, things . . . well . . . *slid* a little in her absence.

"It needs some attention," she says. "But it isn't as horrible as it once was."

Fortunately, he seems receptive. The other day, he was off on a business trip to Boston—and asked her for advice on ties before he left (nonstapled ones, that is).

Remember Christopher, my six-year-old son, who is squeamish about our weekly manicures and pedicures? Last weekend, he was the ring-bearer in a wedding and wore a tuxedo for the first time. He *insisted* on having his nails manicured. He also wanted his hair gelled. He kept his tuxedo jacket on for the entire hour-long ceremony, even though it was 90 degrees out.

Remember Antonio, my ex, with whom I was less-than-supportive about his appearance? He looks great these days. He exercises regularly, and he's chucked the ratty sweats in favor of bicycle shorts (in which he goes on long-distance bike rides all over the countryside).

My man these days—and for the rest of my days, I hope—dresses better than I do. I have never had to sneak into his closet in the middle of the night and throw things out. I have never had to go on shopping sprees for him.

On the other hand, when I first met him, his eating habits were less than stellar. Breakfast usually consisted of a cup of coffee with cream and sugar. Lunch might be a bagel. The only real meal he had was dinner at six or seven, which could be anything from a slice of pizza to steak au poivre at a fancy French restaurant.

But this changed over time. Whenever he spent the night, I served him what *I* always ate for breakfast: nonfat yogurt, fresh fruit, hard-boiled eggs, OJ, coffee. One day, he called me from his apartment and said, "I bought some of that nonfat yogurt for breakfast. It's really good." Stifling my excitement, I said very casually: "Yeah, it is good, isn't it?"

These days, he loves going to our local farmer's market with me and picking out fresh spinach, berries, and other food for our meals. He is an incredible cook, and we enjoy hanging out in the kitchen together.

Exercise is another issue. I go to the gym three or four times a week and I also jog. He is not an exerciser.

But a few weeks ago, when I got home from a run and was describing the tedious details to him *ad nauseum* ("I thought I was going to tank when I got to this hill, but then I got a second wind, and ohmigod, you should have seen me, I started going so fast . . ."), he said, "Maybe I could run with you sometime."

Once again, stifling my excitement, I said very casually, "Yeah, sure. That would be fun."

I am so happy that I have been able to influence and inspire him in these ways . . . just as he has influenced and inspired *me* in so many ways. And I hope that he and I enjoy a long, blissful life together, full of good health and good times and good food and good runs and more.

That being said . . .

I would stand by him no matter what. Even if he gained 50 pounds, got disfiguring scars, or lost all his hair, I would love him and want him to be my man.

Other women seem to share my attitude, either in whole or in part. When I asked women if they would love their man and stand by him no matter how he looked, they wrote:

Absolutely.

You bet!

Now that I know him—absolutely yes.

I hope so.

I married him for the whole package. I love him for what he is and who he is and what he looks like.

Yes, absolutely. I'd love him at 165 pounds where he is now, or at 365.

I think so. I fell in love with the inarticulate dresser, and I love him the same. Except those sneakers with the holes in the toe.

Yes, yes, yes. He's my honey!

And of course, there's the big picture. I mean, the *really* big picture. That is—anytime there is a book, magazine article, talk show, or other forum on the subject of "looking good," there is a dark cloud hovering in the background. That dark cloud is the idea that America has become a "before-and-after" nation; that we value beauty, youth, thinness, and buffness above everything; that we would rather spend our time and money on cosmetic surgery and designer clothes than on other, more noble pursuits.

So the question is: Is it good and healthy and normal—a symbol of our love and devotion, even—if we want to make our men look good? Or are we just caving in to the shallow, superficial values of our times?

"In the 21st century, beauty (or handsomeness) is artillery, and women should be proud to be warriors for beauty," says Ken Siman, author of *The Beauty Trip*. "Are there more important battles in life? Would Winston Churchill have cared about what kind of moisturizer to use after shaving? Would he have put any time into searching for that uncanny personal trainer to learn how to do the perfect crunch? But we're not talking about the beauty of the body versus the beauty of the soul. We're attempting, humbly, to acknowledge the innate allure physical attractiveness holds for all of us, and to embrace it in a time in history when we can take advantage of the leisure, the knowledge, and the technology modernity has afforded us to look—well, *almost*—like the icons of beauty that we all love. When you see a woman who has made a man more than he would be without her, you have seen a true form of love."

Bottom line: Yes, we should never forget what's important in life. And we should never forget what's *truly* important in our relationships with our men. A guy you love and who loves you; who makes you laugh; who is loyal and steadfast; who fusses over you when you are sick; who is the light at the end of the tunnel of each long, long day—those things count way more than a guy who uses just the right aftershave, has great pecs, and knows the difference between a spread collar and a point collar.

I will close with a story from Tess, who talks about her husband, Malcolm:

> When I first met him, he was 6'2" and 170 pounds. He was skinny, skinny, skinny.
>
> But he slowly got more sedentary. This is what a lot of guys do. He's 41 now, middle-aged. And with four kids, food is more of a central part of his life, and exercise, less.
>
> Sure, I'd like to see him more sculpted. But we've been together for 12 years. We don't nag each other about that. It's sort of subtle. If he's put on weight, I say, "I'm going to start running."
>
> I love him no matter what. I love his face. He works so hard. He's a successful businessman and a good father. I know that you can't be everything.
>
> A year or two ago, he was in a funk professionally. And he started looking different. I could tell he was depressed.
>
> So this is what I did. He wanted to make a change. But he had four kids and a wife who didn't work. He had some offers, but they were the same old grind. I encouraged him to take an entrepreneurial job—it was a risky thing that he probably wouldn't have done without my support.
>
> He did it. Now he's happier, more confident. He looks different. He hasn't taken off weight, he isn't dressing differently. But the way he's carrying himself . . . he really looks better. He shines.
>
> I don't nag him. I don't drag him to stores to dress him. If I had my druthers, I'd like it if he were more fashionable.

But I was able to help him look better by helping him find a happier place.

There are middle grounds in life. He's a great husband, a great dad, a great lover, a great provider. Those things matter more than shaving 20 pounds.

Life is about balance. There is no perfection. It's all trade-offs.

In the end, making your man look good is all about loving him, taking care of him, and helping him be the best he can be—inside and out. And hoping that he will do that for you as well. What more can we ask for?